Raphael Semmes
and the *Alabama*

CIVIL WAR CAMPAIGNS AND COMMANDERS SERIES

Under the General Editorship of Grady McWhiney

PUBLISHED

Battle in the Wilderness: Grant Meets Lee by Grady McWhiney
Death in September: The Antietam Campaign
        by Perry D. Jamieson
Texans in the Confederate Cavalry by Anne J. Bailey
Sam Bell Maxey and the Confederate Indians by John C. Waugh
The Saltville Massacre by Thomas D. Mays
General James Longstreet in the West: A Monumental Failure
        by Judith Lee Hallock
The Battle of the Crater by Jeff Kinard
*Cottonclads! The Battle of Galveston and the Defense of the
        Texas Coast* by Donald S. Frazier
A Deep Steady Thunder: The Battle of Chickamauga
        by Steven E. Woodworth
The Texas Overland Expedition of 1863 by Richard Lowe
Raphael Semmes and the Alabama by Spencer C. Tucker

Raphael Semmes
and the *Alabama*

Spencer C. Tucker

Under the General Editorship of Grady McWhiney

McWHINEY
FOUNDATION
PRESS

McMURRY UNIVERSITY
ABILENE, TEXAS

Cataloging-in-Publication Data

Tucker, Spencer, 1937—
    Raphael Semmes and the Alabama / Spencer C. Tucker: under
the general editorship of Grady McWhiney.
        p. cm.
    Includes bibliographical references and index.
    ISBN 1-886661-11-1 (pbk)

    1. Alabama (Ship) 2. United States–History–Civil War,
1861–1865–Naval operations, Confederate. 3. Semmes, Raphael,
1809–1877. 4. Admirals–Confederate States of America–Biography.
5. Confederate States of America. Navy–Biography. I. McWhiney,
Grady. II. Title.

        E599.A3T84 1996
        973.7'57'o92—dc20   95–51436
                                                              CIP

McMurry Station, Box 637
Abilene, TX 79697-0637

Printed in the United States of America

ISBN 1-886661-11-1

10 9 8 7 6 5 4 3 2 1

Book Designed by Rosenbohm Design Group

All inquiries regarding volume purchases of this book should be addressed to
McWhiney Foundation Press, McMurry Station, Box 637, Abilene, TX 79697-0637.
Telephone inquiries may be made by calling (915) 691-6681.

A Note on the Series

Few segments of America's past excite more interest than Civil War battles and leaders. This ongoing series of brief, lively, and authoritative books–*Civil War Campaigns and Commanders*–salutes this passion with inexpensive and accurate accounts that are readable in a sitting. Each volume, separate and complete in itself, nevertheless conveys the agony, glory, death, and wreckage that defined America's greatest tragedy.

In this series, designed for Civil War enthusiasts as well as the newly recruited, emphasis is on telling good stories. Photographs and biographical sketches enhance the narrative of each book, and maps depict events as they happened. Sound history is meshed with the dramatic in a format that is just lengthy enough to inform and yet satisfy.

Grady McWhiney
General Editor

CONTENTS

1. Confederate Commerce Raiding   13

2. Raphael Semmes   18

3. "She Had a Sort of Saucy Air About Her"
   The *Sumter*   24

4. The *Alabama*   31

5. The *Alabama* Begins Cruising   42

6. The *Alabama* and the *Hatteras*   54

7. The *Alabama* Resumes Her Hunt for Prizes   59

8. The *Alabama* and the *Kearsarge*   71

9. After the Battle   91

Appendix:
Prizes Taken by the *Sumter* and the *Alabama*   98

Further Reading   102

Index   107

The brief biographies accompanying the photographs were written by Grady McWhiney and David Coffey.

CAMPAIGNS AND COMMANDERS SERIES

Map Key

Geography

 Trees

Marsh

 Fields

 Strategic Elevations

Rivers

 Tactical Elevations

 Fords

 Orchards

 ——— Political Boundaries

Human Construction

  Bridges

 Railroads

Tactical Towns

● ○ Strategic Towns

□ ■ Buildings

† Church

Roads

Military

  Union Infantry

 Confederate Infantry

 Cavalry

 Artillery

Headquarters

 Encampments

Fortifications

Permanant Works

Hasty Works

Obstructions

 Engagements

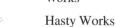 Warships

 Gunboats

 Casemate Ironclad

 Monitor

 Tactical Movements

 Strategic Movements

Maps by
Donald S. Frazier, Ph.D.
Abilene, Texas

MAP

Prizes of the C.S.S. *Alabama*   69

PHOTOGRAPHS AND ILLUSTRATIONS

Stephen R. Mallory	14
Raphael Semmes	19
The C.S.S. *Sumter*	25
James D. Bulloch	32
Charles Francis Adams	34
Arthur F. Sinclair	37
The C.S.S. *Alabama*	38
The *Alabama* burns a prize	43
John McIntosh Kell	46
Some of the officers who served on the *Alabama*	47
Gideon Welles	51
Combat between the *Alabama* and the *Hatteras*	57
Lieutenants Armstrong and Sinclair on deck of the *Alabama*	64
Chart tracking the battle between the *Alabama* and the *Kearsarge*	70
John A. Winslow	74
The U.S.S. *Kearsarge*	75
John Lancaster	78
Spectators viewing action off the coast of Cherbourg, France	79
Combat between the *Alabama* and the *Kearsarge*	85
James S. Thornton	87
The *Deerhound* rescuing survivors of the *Alabama*	88
Raphael Semmes	90

Raphael Semmes and the *Alabama*

1
CONFEDERATE COMMERCE RAIDING

In April 1861 the South was at great disadvantage in most areas, including the naval sphere. Whereas the North began the Civil War with an inadequate naval force (7,600 men and seventy warships, of which forty-two were in commission), the South had virtually no navy at all. In February 1861, when it was organized, the Confederate States Navy had only ten vessels mounting a total of fifty guns. Georgia and South Carolina each supplied two small gunboats and Virginia and North Carolina later transferred five ships to Confederate service, but the total was still less than twenty.

The North also had a very large merchant marine, from which it could draw both ships and seamen, and it possessed extensive shipyards. Eight of ten pre-war navy yards were in the Union.

In this new age of industrial war, machine manufacturing facilities were critical. The North had 85 percent of the factories in the pre-war United States: 119,500 versus only 20,600 for the South. And the gross value of Southern manufactured products was even less—only about one-tenth that of the North. The North used its industrial base to good advantage. Thanks to new manufacture and merchant marine conversions,

Stephen R. Mallory: born Trinidad, West Indies, 1812 or 1813; his family moved to Key West, Florida, in 1820 and two years later his father died; an Episcopalian, Mallory attended school in Mobile, Alabama, and, in 1826, the Moravian School for Boys in Nazareth, Pennsylvania; for seven years, he served as customs inspector in Key West before studying law and being admitted to the bar in 1840; he married Angela Moreno in 1838; they had two daughters and three sons, one of whom followed his father into politics; judge of Monroe County, Florida, from 1840 to 1845, Mallory then became collector of the port of Key West; as his legal reputation grew, he became more active in politics; the Florida legislature sent him to the U.S. Senate in 1851 where he served for ten years and was on the Naval Affairs Committee; converted to secession in 1860, he resigned from the Senate when Florida seceded and moved to his home in Pensacola; named secretary of the navy by President Davis in 1861, Mallory held that position throughout the war; his department received much less attention than the war department, but unlike the secretary of war, who was constantly interfered with by the president, Mallory truly commanded the navy, because Davis knew little about naval affairs; Mallory went to England in 1862 and with the aid of naval agent James D. Bulloch planned war cruisers that drove Federal shipping from the seas; Mallory, who experimented with planned economic warfare, refused to allow Confederate naval vessels to become blockade runners; he believed that the Confederates should concentrate their limited resources on ironclads; as conditions deteriorated, he left Richmond with President Davis and was captured in Georgia in May 1865; after his release from prison in March 1866, Mallory practiced law in Pensacola until his death in 1873.

by 1865 the U.S. Navy had seven hundred vessels of all types, including sixty ironclads. This made the U.S. Navy second in size in the world only to Great Britain.

Confederate Secretary of the Navy Stephen Russell Mallory knew that seapower would have a considerable impact on the war's outcome. He also knew that the South did not have the means of creating a navy in its own territory. In 1861 the South had no facilities for constructing even moderate-sized warships.

The firing on Fort Sumter on April 12, 1861, led U.S. President Abraham Lincoln to call for 75,000 volunteers. On April 17, two days after Lincoln's call for volunteers, Confederate States President Jefferson Davis issued a proclamation inviting applications for letters of marque and reprisal (a step confirmed by the Confederate Congress on May 6). This action authorized Southern private vessels ("privateers") to take Union ships. In retaliation, on April 19 Lincoln proclaimed a blockade of Confederate coasts and warned that anyone attacking a U.S. vessel would be treated as a pirate. This threat did not deter numerous applications for letters of marque from Southern cities and as far away as Great Britain.

The use of privately owned volunteer cruisers, known as privateers, to attack enemy shipping was hardly new. Americans had sent large numbers of them to sea in the War of the American Revolution and especially in the War of 1812. The U.S. Navy had also devoted itself largely to commerce raiding (the *guerre de course* as it came to be known) in both conflicts. For the Confederacy the situation was analogous to these earlier American wars: a nation weak on the seas facing a far more powerful foe with a formidable fleet and an extensive and vulnerable merchant marine.

If the Confederacy were able to strike a strong blow at Union merchant shipping it would wound the North financially and might weaken Northern resolve. Even modest successes would force up insurance rates and minimize profits. And even a few raiders would probably force the U.S. Navy to shift warships from blockade duties.

Although the first Confederate privateers initially found easy hunting, most were gone within a year. The Union blockade made it difficult for them to bring their prizes into Southern ports and many privateers were simply converted into blockade runners. The South faced another difficulty as well. On May 14 Great Britain declared her neutrality and over the next several months France, Spain, the Netherlands, and Brazil followed suit. This meant there were very few places to which captured vessels might be sailed and sold. As a result most U.S. merchantmen taken by the Confederates as prizes were burned.

There were important voices in the Confederacy favoring concentrating on small sailing vessels for the war against Union commerce. Large steamers were expensive and purchasing only a few seemed like putting all one's eggs in one basket. The cruisers would also face another daunting problem, lack of a secure supply base. As Commander Matthew Fontaine Maury put it, they would not have "a friendly port in the wide world." Maury's fears proved unfounded; despite difficulties, Confederate commerce raiders got the coal and other supplies they needed.

Correctly, Mallory decided against the smaller vessels. To continue the war against Union commerce the Confederacy turned to government owned and financed commerce raiders. Such ships had to be specially designed for their mission. They would be steamers. But steamers of that day were hermaphrodites; given their limited coal storage capacity they carried full sail rigs and used them almost exclusively for cruising. Steaming was usually reserved for close-in maneuvering. The raiders would also need to be roomy enough to carry large crews and supplies for extended voyages. They would also need space for captured crews.

To find these ships the South turned to foreign ship yards,

notably those of Great Britain. And to head the task of over-
seas procurement of warships, Mallory turned to James
Dunwoody Bulloch. Mallory sent him to Britain to obtain ships.
He instructed Bulloch to get such ships to sea as quickly as
possible in order to destroy Union commerce and cause the
U.S. Navy to detach its own warships to pursue them. The
Alabama was only one of a number of such vessels.

2
RAPHAEL SEMMES

Depending on one's point of view, the C.S.S. *Alabama* was either the most successful or the most notorious of Civil War Confederate commerce raiders. During the war no fewer than a dozen such ships attacked Union merchantmen, but the *Alabama's* toll of Union vessels taken, sixty-six (her tender, the ex-*Conrad*, took two more), nearly equaled the combined total of the two next most successful raiders: the *Shenandoah* and the *Florida*. The *Shenandoah* (Captain James T. Waddell) took thirty-eight prizes; the *Florida* (Captain John N. Maffit) captured thirty-three, and her prizes *Tacony* and *Clarence* took twenty-three more.

If the *Alabama* was by far the best known of Confederate commerce raiders, her captain, Raphael Semmes, was easily the most feared and notorious of Confederate naval commanders.

Raphael Semmes—naval captain, improvisor, and diplomat—was neither a large man nor physically impressive. An

Raphael Semmes: born Maryland 1809; began his naval career as a midshipmen in 1826; during leaves he studied law and in 1834 was admitted to the Maryland bar; commissioned a lieutenant in 1837, Semmes commanded blockading vessels during the Mexican War; when his ship, the *Somers*, sank, he barely escaped death; he authored two books on the war: *The Campaign of General Scott and Service Afloat and Ashore During the Mexican War*; in 1849 he moved to Mobile, Alabama, and became inspector of lighthouses along the Gulf Coast; promoted to commander in 1855 and placed in charge of the Navy's Lighthouse Bureau, a position he held until 1861; Semmes resigned from the U.S. Navy soon after Alabama seceded; he first served the Confederacy by purchasing munitions and supplies in the North; after the war began, he became a commander in the Confederate Navy and assigned to head the Lighthouse Bureau; soon he received permission to convert the *Havana* into a commerce raider; renaming his ship the *Sumter* in June 1861, Semmes began a cruise of six months dur-

ing which he captured eighteen prizes; Federal vessels eventually blockaded the Sumter in Gibraltar, but Semmes escaped to England and took command of the C.S.S. *Alabama*; promoted to captain in 1862, he sailed from England, roaming the oceans in search of prizes; in two years he captured sixty-six vessels; the U.S.S. *Kearsage* finally sank the *Alabama* off Cherbourg, France, in 1864, but Semmes was rescued by a yacht and taken to England; returning to the Confederacy, he was promoted to rear admiral in February 1865 and placed in command of the James River Squadron; after Richmond fell, Semmes destroyed his ships and moved westward with his sailors; President Davis appointed "Old Beeswax," as his men called him, a brigadier general and directed him to defend Danville, Virginia; when Confederate forces surrendered, Semmes insisted that his parole list him both as a rear admiral and a brigadier general; he emphasized that his army rank be included on his parole to prevent any attempt to try him as a naval "pirate" for his raiding activities; Semmes returned to Mobile after the war, briefly serving as county probate judge, but Reconstruction officials removed him from office; for a time he taught moral philosophy at the Louisiana Military Institute (later Louisiana State University) and edited a Memphis newspaper; he returned to Mobile in 1868 to practice law; he died in 1877 and is buried in the Mobile Catholic Cemetery.

introvert who did not socialize with his officers, Semmes exercised leadership of the quiet and calm variety, but to his supporters it was unquestioned. As James Bulloch put it, "If circumstances had ever placed him at the head of a fleet, I feel sure he would have achieved important and notable results." In his *Naval History of the Civil War*, outspoken and partisan U.S. Navy Admiral David Porter expressed an opposite view. He called Semmes "perhaps the most vindictive of all the officers of the Confederate Navy." Porter also wrote that "while in the United States Navy, Semmes had little reputation as an officer. He had no particular taste for his profession....He was indolent and fond of his comfort, so that altogether his associates in the Navy gave him credit for very little energy." Probably the truth lies somewhere between these two extremes; certainly Semmes was a competent naval officer. He was also, on occasion, extremely lucky.

Semmes was born on September 27, 1809, in Charles County, Maryland, of French Catholic ancestry. His parents died early in his childhood and he was raised in Georgetown, District of Columbia, by an uncle and aunt. In April 1826 President Adams appointed Semmes, at age sixteen, a midshipman in the Navy. Although he performed well and was second in his class in a course at the naval school at the Gosport Navy Yard, there were too many U.S. Navy officers and promotion was slow; thus it was February 1837 before Semmes made lieutenant. Encouraged to take leaves of absence, he spent considerable time ashore and began to study law, a profession he followed when he was not at sea. In 1834 he was admitted to the Maryland bar and in 1837 he married Anne E. Spencer. She and their six children survived him.

From 1837 until the Mexican War Semmes spent most of his time on survey work along the Southern coast and the Gulf of Mexico. In 1841 he was ordered on a survey of Ship Island and the surrounding waters of Mississippi Sound. He took his family with him and at that time established his legal residence in Alabama.

With the Mexican War in October 1846 Semmes was appointed to command the unlucky brig *Somers* on blockade duties. Launched in 1841, in November 1842 the *Somers*, commanded by martinet Captain A.S. Mackenzie, was returning from Africa when a mutiny was discovered. Three individuals were executed aboard ship on scanty evidence; they included the alleged ringleader and son of the secretary of war, 19-year-old Midshipman Philip Spencer. Despite efforts to hush it up, the affair caused a national scandal when the brig returned to the United States.

On December 8, 1846, the *Somers* went down in only ten minutes from a sudden squall while off the eastern coast of Mexico and half of her crew was lost. Semmes and the remainder were rescued by a British warship. A court martial acquitted Semmes of any blame and its officers even commended him on his seamanship.

In March 1847 Semmes went ashore with naval artillery at Vera Cruz and took part in its bombardment, having charge of guns landed from the *Raritan*. He also participated in the expedition against Tuxpan and was detailed on special duty to accompany General Winfield Scott's army to Mexico City. During the march to the Mexican interior, Semmes served as a volunteer aide to division commander Major General William Worth, who on several occasions cited him for bravery.

After the war Semmes found himself in the familiar situation of being in a navy with too many officers and spent much of his time on awaiting-orders status. In November 1847 he returned to his home on the Perdido River, in Alabama, near Pensacola, Florida, where he had established his family in 1845. In October 1849 he moved his residence to near Mobile.

In 1852 Semmes published *Service Afloat and Ashore During the Mexican War*, a book about his Mexican War experiences. Interestingly, in it Semmes argued that if Mexico had fitted out privateers to prey on U.S. shipping they should have been treated as pirates. The book was well received and

helped to establish both his law practice and entrance into
Mobile politics. In 1855 Semmes was promoted to commander
and a year later was assigned to Washington as naval secretary of the Lighthouse Board. While there he made the
acquaintance of Senator Jefferson Davis from Mississippi.

Following his state's secession and creation of the
Confederate States of America, on February 15, 1861,
Semmes resigned his commission in the U.S. Navy and went to
Montgomery, Alabama, to present his views on defense mat-
ters to the Confederacy's Committee on Naval Affairs. Shortly
thereafter President Davis sent him into the North to purchase
military and naval supplies as well as equipment with which to
improve the Tredegar Iron Works at Richmond. During his
absence in March Semmes was appointed a commander in the
Confederate States Navy. On April 4 he returned to
Montgomery and was appointed chief of the Light-House
Bureau. After the shelling of Fort Sumter, Semmes, in his
words, "at once sought an interview with the Secretary of the
Navy Mallory, and explained to him my desire to get afloat."

Semmes had already been thinking in terms of striking
against Union commerce. Before the firing on Sumter, Semmes
had received a letter from a member of the Congress from the
South seeking his views on naval policy should there be war,
and Semmes had replied:

> You ask me to explain what I mean, by an irregu-
> lar naval force. I mean a well-organized system of
> private armed ships, called privateers. If you are
> warred upon at all, it will be by a commercial people,
> whose ability to do you harm will consist chiefly in
> ships, and shipping. It is at ships and shipping,
> therefore, that you must strike; and the most effectu-
> al way to do this, is, by means of the irregular force
> of which I speak.

With few ships available, commerce raiding seemed the only real way the South could strike a blow at the Union and Semmes was eager to do just that.

3

"SHE HAD A SORT OF SAUCY AIR ABOUT HER" THE *SUMTER*

Semmes found in Secretary Mallory a kindred spirit, a strong advocate of commerce raiding. Mallory, however, gave a gloomy assessment of available vessels but shared with Semmes the reports on each. Semmes quickly asked for, and received the next day (April 18), command of the *Habana* at New Orleans. A steamer packet of 437 tons with coal capacity sufficient for only five days, she had been launched in 1857 and had been employed on the New Orleans to Havana route. Renamed the *Sumter* in honor of the recent Confederate victory and commissioned on June 3, she was the first Confederate Navy commerce raider.

Semmes described the *Sumter* in these words: "I found her

The C.S.S. *Sumter*

only a dismantled packet-ship, full of upper cabins, and other top-hamper, furniture, and crockery, but as unlike a ship of war as possible. Still, I was pleased with her general appearance. Her lines were easy and graceful, and she had a sort of saucy air about her which seemed to say that she was not averse to the service of which she was about to be employed."

Semmes personally oversaw conversion of the *Sumter* into a warship. There was no end to difficulties in fitting out the ship and even Porter grudgingly concluded that Semmes did an outstanding job: "the patience and energy he exhibited were worthy of a better cause." The *Sumter* was first stripped down to what would be her gun deck, which was then reinforced. She also received additional coal bunkers. Mallory issued orders that arming the *Sumter* was to receive top priority. Her guns, taken from recently captured U.S. Navy stocks, were shipped, not without difficulty, via rail from the Gosport (Norfolk), Virginia, navy yard to New Orleans.

The *Sumter*'s armament consisted of an 8-inch "shell gun" (intended to fire primarily eight-inch diameter explosive-filled shells) and four 32-pounders (firing solid shot of that weight). The weight of the guns themselves was usually expressed in "hundredweight" (cwt) or 112-pound units, and these "shot guns" were extraordinarily light for the size of shot they threw, weighing only twenty-seven cwt or about 3,000 pounds each: they would not be able to fire the heavy charge of powder necessary to send shot at high velocity. In addition they were broadside-mounted, on carriages along the ship's sides. This gave them only limited traverse (ability to turn from side to side so as to cover a wide extent of sea). In contrast, the 8-inch gun was placed on a pivot mount amidships—an arrangement increasingly in favor on steamers for long-range fire by large guns, since it provided a wide traverse. In a pivot mount the gun and its carriage were set on two parallel tracks, known as "skids," held in place by three or more cross members. The gun, its carriage, and the skids on which it recoiled, traversed to port or starboard by being rotated around a metal bolt, which passed through the central cross member and a metal collar in the ship's deck. The cannon was then loaded, run out, fired, and recoiled back on the skids.

The *Sumter* was rerigged as a barkentine (a three-masted sailing vessel but square-rigged on the foremast only; the main and mizzen masts were rigged fore-and-aft) and Semmes signed on a crew of 114 officers and men. New Orleans was full of seamen from ships that had been laid up thanks to the Union naval blockade, and Semmes had the great advantage of being able to pick those he wanted. Although their pay was only slightly higher than that given ordinary navy seamen, the men received gold rather than Confederate script, the South's inflation-prone emergency paper money; their chief incentive, however, was the possibility of sharing in prize money.

On June 18, 1861, Semmes ran the *Sumter* down the Mississippi past Forts Jackson and St. Philip to the river's mouth to await a favorable moment to escape two blockading Union warships: the side-wheel frigate *Powhatan* (one XI-inch Dahlgren smoothbore, ten IX-inch Dahlgrens, and five 12-pounder howitzers; Commander David D. Porter) and the powerful screw sloop *Brooklyn* (twenty-four IX-inch Dahlgrens and two 12-pounder howitzers; Commander Charles Poor). The moment came on June 30, when the *Brooklyn* was some eight miles to westward, pursuing another ship. As soon as black smoke was detected from the *Sumter*, the *Brooklyn* sought to return to her anchorage, but she had the current against her whereas the *Sumter* had the current in her favor. In her dash to the bar the *Sumter* managed to outrun the *Brooklyn* off Pass à l'Outre in what Porter called "one of the most exciting chases of the war" (although Porter did chide the captain of the *Brooklyn* for not attempting at least ricochet firing from his bow chasers when his quarry was within range). It was a near-run thing; at one point Semmes had ordered the paymaster to prepare to throw his iron chest and all its contents overboard.

The *Sumter* was now free to roam the Gulf. Mallory's orders to Semmes were, "do the enemy's commerce the greatest injury in the shortest time."

On July 3 the *Sumter* took her first prize, a merchant bark (a three-masted sailing vessel, square-rigged on the fore and main masts, fore-and-aft on the mizzen). The procedure followed was the same for the many captures to come. The *Sumter*, flying a British flag, overhauled the bark, which from her lines was thought to be American. Semmes ordered a gun fired and the bark then hoisted the U.S. flag. Semmes then ordered the Confederate flag hoisted on his own ship and sent a boat to the other vessel with a boarding officer. He returned with the bark's captain and her papers. The vessel turned out to be the nearly new *Golden Rocket*, worth between $30,000 and $40,000. As Semmes noted, "There were no knotty points of fact or law to embarrass my decision. There were the American register, and clearance, and the American character impressed upon every plank and spar of the ship." Once her U.S. registry had been determined, the *Golden Rocket* was doomed. Semmes informed her captain that he would be destroying the bark but that the crew would be well treated aboard his own vessel. Semmes later wrote in his memoirs, "Boats were then dispatched to bring off the crew, and such provisions, cordage, sails, and paints as the different departments of my ship stood in need of, and at about ten-o'clock at night, the order was given to apply the torch to her." Semmes wrote in his journal at the time: "Our first prize made a beautiful bonfire and we did not enjoy the spectacle the less because she was from the black Republican State of Maine." Porter called the *Golden Rocket* "the first illegal prize made by a Confederate vessel-of-war."

Semmes also discovered that neutrality laws limited the time Confederate cruisers might spend in port and prohibited their captains from improving their vessels' fighting characteristics; the only authorized repairs were those restoring seaworthiness. As a result he and his crews became masters at deception.

Captive seamen aboard ship were also a problem and a danger. Semmes would often transfer captured crews and passengers to willing neutral ships or to Union merchant ships carrying a cargo belonging to a neutral. Occasionally a ship would be let go on bond—that is, the captain signed a paper guaranteeing to pay a set sum to the Confederate government at the end of the war—to carry passengers.

Over the next six months Semmes cruised the Caribbean, capturing nine other vessels. He sailed the *Sumter* along the South American coast to Brazil and then back to the West Indies but found only two U.S. registered vessels, both of which he burned. The absence of other U.S. vessels convinced him that he would do better in European waters and he took the *Sumter* into the Atlantic. Late in November the *Sumter* narrowly escaped an encounter with the more powerful U.S. Navy screw sloop *Iroquois* (two XI-inch Dahlgren smoothbores and four 32-pounder 42cwt smoothbores). During the crossing Semmes took six Union prizes.

On January 3 the *Sumter*, in poor repair, put into Cádiz. Spanish authorities allowed Semmes to make only repairs rather than the engine overhaul he wanted. They then ordered him to depart and Semmes did so. On the eighteenth he took two prizes, and a day later arrived at Gibraltar. There British authorities were much more gracious than the chilly Spanish officials at Cádiz, but U.S. Consul Horatio J. Sprague managed to block the sale of coal to the Confederate warship and, in the meantime, U.S. Navy warships, including the screw sloop *Kearsarge*, arrived to wait for the *Sumter* to come out. Since his ship needed repairs to her boilers and hull for which facilities were not available at Gibraltar, Semmes bowed to the inevitable. With the permission of Confederate commissioner James M. Mason in London, Semmes laid up the *Sumter* at Gibraltar in April, paid off most of her crew, and left for

London, expecting to sail for home from there. In December 1862 the *Sumter* was sold at Gibraltar at auction to a British firm, which put her back into commercial service under the name *Gibraltar*.

Although the *Sumter* was too small and too slow to be an effective commerce raider, Semmes had established his reputation. He had managed to outwit the captains of Union warships sent to intercept him, he had divined the location of enemy merchantmen, and he had been successful in securing admittance to neutral ports.

The *Sumter* had also taken eighteen prizes, two of which were recaptured with their prize crews: one was retaken from the prize crew by their Union captives and the other when it failed to run the naval blockade before New Orleans. Semmes burned seven ships; another seven were returned by Cuban authorities to their Union owners. On August 21, 1862, the Confederate Congress promoted Semmes captain and on September 9 voted him special thanks, although it was many months before the news reached him.

Semmes had already sailed for home. He was at Nassau where he hoped to catch a blockade runner to the South when Commander Terry Sinclair brought orders from Mallory for him to return to England to take command of a ship contracted for by Captain Bulloch and nearing completion at the Birkenhead Ironworks, Liverpool.

4
THE *ALABAMA*

James Bulloch was the most effective Confederate agent abroad. After the April 1861 firing on Fort Sumter Bulloch, a former U.S. Navy officer with fourteen years' service and then captain of a New York mail steamer, telegraphed the Confederate capital to offer his services. After Bulloch's arrival in Montgomery, Mallory ordered him to Europe to buy ships. He arrived in Liverpool in June 1861 and turned out to be worth more to the Confederacy than most of its generals.

Shortly after his July 4, 1861, arrival at Liverpool, Bulloch placed an order with W. C. Miller and Sons for a ship supposedly for the Italian Government and called the *Oreto*. Later she was known as the *Manassas* and finally as the *Florida*. On August 1, 1861, Bulloch commissioned another vessel. The order, placed to his personal account, was with a firm on the other side of the Mersey River, the Birkenhead Ironworks, owned by the firm of John Laird and Sons. Identified in the dockyard as Hull No. 290, the vessel was known when launched on May 15 as the *Enrica*; later she was commissioned the C.S.S. *Alabama*.

Bulloch not only arranged for cruisers; he organized shipments of war supplies to the Confederacy and acquired blockade runners. Bulloch purchased 13,000 Enfield rifles, stores of ammunition, several pieces of artillery, uniforms, and medical supplies, and then personally ran them all through the blockade to the Confederacy in the *Fingal*. The first Confederate government-owned blockade runner (too many private ships mere-

James D. Bulloch: born Georgia 1823, to Major James Stephens and Hester Amarinthia (Elliott) Bulloch, daughter of U.S. Senator John Elliott; enlisted as a midshipman in the U.S. Navy in 1839, sailed on the *United States*, and was sta-

tioned off the coast of Brazil on the *Potomac*; in 1842 Bulloch cruised the Mediterranean in the ship of the line *Delaware*; he attended naval school in Philadelphia in 1844-1845, graduating second in his class; stationed off the Pacific Coast during the Mexican War, he later commanded the *Georgia*, the first subsidized mail steamer to California; assigned to the U.S. Coastal Survey from 1849 to 1851; he married Elizabeth Euphemia Caskie in 1851; she died in 1854; he married Mrs. Harriett Cross Foster in 1857; Bulloch entered the Confederate Navy as a commander; he requested a line assignment, but his talents were considered too valuable and instead the government sent him as a naval agent to England where he attempted to buy or build naval vessels; after furnishing the Confederacy with the English cruisers *Florida*, *Alabama*, and *Shenandoah*, and the French ram *Stonewall*, Bulloch aided in Confederate diplomatic negotiations; after the war, unable to secure a pardon from the Federals, he remained in Liverpool, England, where he entered the mercantile business and became a scholar and master of maritime and international law; he published *The Secret Service of the Confederate States in Europe* (1884). Bulloch died in Liverpool in 1901.

ly carried products that would return the highest profits rather than essential war supplies), the *Fingal* reached Savannah with more war supplies than any other ship that ran the Civil War blockade. Later she was converted into the ram *Atlanta*.

Mallory had led Bulloch to believe that he would have command of the first vessel completed in Britain (the *Florida*), but in his absence she had gone to Maffit. Bulloch expected to have the second command and had even made arrangements with Maffit for a joint cruise with the *Florida*. But Semmes was without a ship and in early July word came from Richmond that he would get the new vessel while Bulloch worked to secure ironclads (the "Laird Rams").

During her building there was much discussion concerning the ultimate disposition of hull 290. It was obvious to any trained observer that she had been specially designed for speedy conversion into an armed cruiser. The name of her purchaser was secret, but the British Government was well aware of what was going on.

With the *Florida* already at sea, Thomas H. Dudley, the U.S. Consul at Liverpool, hired a private detective, Matthew Maguire, to find out more about the mysterious hull and determine its ultimate disposition. U.S. Minister Charles Francis Adams repeatedly addressed notes of complaint to the British Government about the *Enrica*.

Six Confederate cruisers were built in Great Britain: the *Alabama*, *Chickamauga*, *Florida*, *Georgia*, *Shenandoah*, and *Tallahassee*. To circumvent neutrality laws all sailed without armament and received it elsewhere. This was only a transparent cover and the British Government knew the true situation. As historian J. Russell Soley noted,

Among the innumerable side-issues presented by the case of the *Alabama*, the facts...contain the essential point. That the attention of the British Government was called to the suspicious character of the vessel on the 23d of June; that her adaptation to warlike use was admitted; that her readiness for sea was well known; that evidence was submitted on the 21st, the 23d, and finally on the 25th of July, that put her character beyond a doubt; and that, in spite of all this, she was allowed to sail on the 29th, make the real foundation of the case against Great Britain.

The inference is unavoidable that the Government deliberately intended to pursue a policy as unfriendly as it could possibly be without passing the technical bounds of a legal neutrality.

Charles Francis Adams: born Massachusetts 1807, the son of President John Quincy Adams and grandson of President John Adams; after spending much of his childhood abroad, Charles Adams entered Harvard College, from which he was graduated in 1825; he studied law in Boston and was admitted to the bar in 1829; he also developed an interest in history and wrote for several journals; in 1840 he edited and published the letters of his grandmother, Abigail Adams; that same year he was elected to the Massachusetts legislature as a Whig; he was also by this time a leading opponent of slavery, having earlier been ambivalent; from 1850–1856 he

devoted himself almost entirely to the publication of the ten-volume *Works of John Adams*; in 1858 he won election as a Republican to the U.S. House of Representatives, filling his father's former seat; in 1861 he was appointed minister to Great Britain, where he worked to prevent British recognition of the Confederacy; he almost immediately had to deal with the political fallout caused by the *Trent* affair and the threat of direct British intervention; he worked to insure British neutrality and protested ship building contracts and other arms sales to the Confederacy; in the closing stages of the war Adams began to press the case of Britain's liability for losses to United States commerce resulting from Confederate raiders using ships of British origin; he returned to the U. S. in 1868, but was recalled three years later to arbitrate in the *Alabama* claims case; he then returned to his family's papers, publishing the *Memoirs of John Quincy Adams*; he died at Boston in 1886.

Later the British Government paid dearly for its duplicitous role.

By adroit maneuvering Bulloch was able to skirt the Foreign Enlistment Act of 1819, which prohibited any British citizen from equipping, furnishing, fitting out, or arming any vessel intended for service by foreign belligerent navies. Bulloch obtained help from eminent Liverpool lawyer F. S. Hull, who assisted with the act's intricacies. Hull claimed that "the mere building of a ship within Her Majesty's dominions...is no offence, *whatever may be the intent of the parties*, because the offense is not the *building* but the *equipping*.*" Bulloch took care to see that none of the cruisers he had built in Britain went to sea with ordnance, small arms, or warlike stores of any kind. These he obtained and shipped in other vessels so the cruisers could be outfitted in international waters. The *Florida* was outfitted in the Bahamas and the *Alabama* in the Azores; Bulloch picked the latter site from having stopped there in the *Fingal*.

On June 15 the *Enrica* made a successful trial cruise. During July, Minister Adams presented additional damning evidence that left no doubt as to the ship's true nature and purpose to Robert P. Collier, judge advocate for the British fleet and an authority on maritime law. Collier was convinced that the *Enrica* was in violation of British law. It was his opinion that if the ship were allowed to sail the U.S. government would have "serious grounds of complaint." Adams then took this opinion to British Foreign Secretary John Earl Russell, and he agreed to take the case up with Sir John Harding, the queen's advocate. Fortunately for the Confederates Harding suffered a crippling stroke and his wife allowed the materials to remain unopened for three days. At the same time Adams ordered Captain T.A. Craven, commander of the U.S.S. *Tuscarora*, then at Southampton, to intercept the *Enrica* if she put to sea.

On July 26 Bulloch received word "from a private but most reliable source" that he had best get his ship out of the Mersey

River in less than forty-eight hours if he expected to prevent her being impounded by the British Government. Bulloch was also warned that the *Tuscarora* was looking for the *Enrica*. Much has been written about this warning to Bulloch; there is speculation that it came from someone in the British government. Later Bulloch strongly defended Price Edwards, a local British official, against charges that he was the individual who had aided the Confederate cruiser's escape. When British Foreign Secretary Russell finally acted on his own and sent an order to detain the *Enrica*, it arrived after she had sailed.

On receiving the warning, Bulloch immediately informed the Lairds that he wanted to carry out another trial run, and he had a skeleton crew and a British master, Captain Mathew J. Butcher, come on board. To add to the illusion, on the morning of July 29 Bulloch invited guests aboard and had the ship dressed out in flags as if for an excursion. The steam tug *Hercules* went along as tender. After lunch Bulloch informed his guests that he had decided to leave the ship out all night, and that afternoon he returned with them to Liverpool in the tug. He also told the pilot to take the *Enrica* to Point Lynas, about fifty miles away, where she anchored. Early the next morning Bulloch was back aboard the *Hercules* with additional crewmen for the *Enrica*. As they left Liverpool Bulloch was handed a telegram with news that the *Tuscarora* had departed Southampton to search for the *Enrica*, probably toward Queenstown on the southern Irish coast. This news caused Bulloch to change the *Enrica*'s route. Instead of sailing south she would head north into the Irish Sea. Bulloch left the *Enrica* off the Giant's Causeway after ordering Captain Butcher to sail her around Ireland to Terceira Island in the Azores.

The *Agrippina* sailed at the same time, carrying the future commerce raider's ordnance, ammunition, stores, and 250 tons of coal. On 13 August Bulloch and Semmes (who had arrived in Liverpool a few days after the *Enrica* sailed) and other officers left Liverpool aboard the *Bahama*. Semmes brought along his extensive law library, which would be useful in adjudicating condemnation cases.

The *Enrica* arrived at Porto Praia da Vitória, Terceira, in the Azores on August 9. Portuguese officials were told she was the *Barcelona*, bound from London to Havana for the Spanish Government. The *Agrippina* arrived on August 18 and two days later the *Bahama* came up.

Semmes ordered the three vessels to Angra Bay on the lee side of the island, where the water was smoother, and he set foot on the *Enrica* for the first time. Here, "beyond the marine league" (three nautical miles, i.e., in international waters), the *Enrica* took on coal. At the same time the crew transferred stores and ordnance. Lieutenant Arthur Sinclair described the activity:

The carpenter and mates assisted by the engineers were measuring and putting down the "circles" for the two pivot-guns. The boatswain and mates fitting train and side-tackles to the broadside guns. Gunner stowing the magazine, shot and shot lockers. Sailmaker looking after his spare sails, and seeing them safely stored in the sailroom....Day and night on goes the work: each hour the 290 looking more like a man-of-war....

Arthur F. Sinclair: became a midshipman in the U.S. Navy in 1823; passed midshipman in 1831; promoted to lieutenant in 1835 and to commander in 1855; dismissed in 1861. Sinclair served on the Alabama during its entire journey and survived the battle with the Kearsarge, years later he wrote a valuable book on his experiences, *Two Years on the Alabama*, published in 1895.

The C.S.S. *Alabama*

On August 24 in international waters, to the tune of "Dixie" and salutes, Semmes commissioned his new command the *Alabama*. Across her wheel in gilded carving were the words, "Aide toi et Dieu t'aidera" (French for "Heaven helps those who help themselves").

Semmes and his officers then donned dress uniforms and mustered the crews of the *Agrippina* and *Bahama*. After a rousing speech Semmes persuaded some eighty men to sign on. It was probably not a difficult sell. They were promised double standard wages in gold and prize money to be appropriated by the Confederate Congress for any ships they destroyed. There were no living expenses. Semmes turned over the financial arrangements regarding the crew to Bulloch who then sailed back to Liverpool in the *Bahama*.

The *Alabama* was a sleek, three-masted, bark-rigged sloop built of oak with a copper hull. Semmes described her as "a very perfect ship of her class":

> She was of about 900 tons burden, 230 feet in length, 32 feet in breadth, 20 feet in depth, and drew, when provisioned and coaled for a cruise, 15 feet of water. Her model was of the most perfect symmetry, and she sat upon the water with the lightness and grace of a swan. She was barkentine rigged, with long lower masts, which enabled her to carry large fore-and-aft sails, as jibs and try-sails, which are of so much importance to a steamer, in so many emergencies. Her sticks were of the best yellow pine that would bend in a gale, like a willow wand, without breaking, and her rigging was of the best of Swedish iron wire. The scantling of the vessel was light, compared with other vessels of her class in the Federal Navy, but this was scarcely a disadvantage as she was designed as a scourge of the enemy's commerce, rather than for battle. She was to defend herself,

simply, if defence should become necessary. Her engine was of three hundred horse-power, and she had attached an apparatus for condensing, from the vapor of seawater, all the fresh water that her crew might require. She was a perfect steamer and a perfect sailing-ship, at the same time, neither of her two modes of locomotion being at all dependent upon the other....the *Sumter*, when her fuel was exhausted, was little better than a log on the water, because of the inability to hoist her propellers which she was, in consequence, compelled to drag after her. The *Alabama* was so constructed, that in fifteen minutes, her propeller could be detached from the shaft and lifted in a well contrived for the purpose, sufficiently high out of the water, not to be an impediment to her speed. When this was done, and her sails spread, she was to all intents and purposes, a sailing-ship. On the other hand, when I desired to use her as a steamer, I had only to start the fires, lower the propeller, and if the wind was adverse, brace her yards to the wind, and the conversion was complete. The speed of the *Alabama* was always greatly over-rated by the enemy. She was ordinarily about a ten-knot ship. She was said to have made eleven knots and a half, on her trial trip, but we never afterward got it out of her. Under steam and sail both, we logged on one occasion thirteen knots and a quarter; which was her utmost speed.

Her armament consisted of eight guns; six 32-pounders, in broadside, and two pivot-guns amidships; one on the forecastle, and the other abaft the main-mast—the former a 100-pounder rifled Blakeley, and the latter, a smooth-bore eight-inch. The Blakeley gun was so deficient in metal, compared with the weight of shot it threw, that after the first few discharges, when it became a little heated, it was of comparatively little use to us, to such an extent that we were obliged to reduce the charge of powder, on account of the recoil. The average crew of the *Alabama*, before the mast, was about 120 men; and she carried twenty-four officers, as follows: A Captain, four lieutenants, surgeon, paymaster, master, marine officer, four engineers, two midshipmen, and four master's mates, a Captain's clerk, boatswain, gunner, sailmaker, and carpenter. The cost of the ship, with everything complete, was two hundred and fifty thousand dollars.

The *Alabama*'s six 32-pounders were heavy guns; each weighed 55cwt. Her rifled Blakeley was actually a 7-inch (110-pounder) and the other pivot gun was a smoothbore 8-inch, 68-pounder gun mounted amidships. Her weight of broadside metal was thus 274 pounds (three broadside guns plus the two pivots).

The *Alabama* was a superb example of the shipbuilder's art; John Laird had boasted that she was "the finest cruiser of her class in the world." She carried a large spread of canvas high, and friend and foe alike could identify her from her exceptionally lofty rigging. The *Alabama* was unusual in that she had a fully equipped machine shop to enable her crew to make all ordinary repairs themselves. She carried sufficient coal for eighteen days continuous steaming, although Semmes preferred to rely on sail where possible. In fact, all but about a half dozen of her captures were made under sail alone. Commodious to carry a large crew and supplies for extended cruising, the *Alabama* also had the additional space necessary to house captured crews. If she could reprovision from captured prizes, she would be able to remain at sea a very long time. This was exactly what Semmes intended to do.

5
THE *ALABAMA* BEGINS CRUISING

After a brief shakedown cruise the *Alabama* took her first prize vessels in the vicinity of the Azores; all were American whalers finishing their season there. Her first prize, taken on September 5, was the *Ocmulgee* from Massachusetts. She was an easy capture; when the *Alabama* came up the *Ocmulgee* was lying to with a large whale alongside, which her crew was cutting apart. Nonetheless, the *Alabama* approached under false flag. Only when the American ship had replied with the U.S. flag did Semmes order the Confederate ensign hoisted. This would remain standard practice throughout the *Alabama*'s life as a commerce raider. Semmes would present his ship as a British or Dutch vessel, or even as a U.S. Navy warship. Semmes took the *Ocmulgee*'s crew of thirty-seven men on board as well as some of her stores. The next morning he had

The *Alabama* burns a prize

her burned. Earlier he had ordered her chronometer and flag removed, thus beginning a collection of these items from each vessel he captured.

Semmes transported the *Ocmulgee's* crew to nearby Flores Island, where he sent the men ashore in their own whaleboats. In two weeks in the Azores the *Alabama* took and burned ten prizes: eight whalers, one schooner, and one supply ship. After taking off such supplies and merchandise as might be useful for his own crew, Semmes burned the vast majority of them (a full list of the ships taken is in the appendix). On occasion a captured vessel was also used for target practice. In retrospect Semmes would have done well to have conducted target practice more often but, uncertain of resupply, he thought it best to conserve his ammunition and powder.

The captured vessel's captain was usually allowed one trunk, the mates and men one bag of clothing each. If land was close, Semmes usually put crews and passengers of his prizes into their ships' boats and they rowed these to reach shore. If no land was nearby those taken might be kept on board the *Alabama* or their own vessel for a time before being released; others were set free if Semmes was forced to bond their ships.

Apparently Semmes did what he could to make his prisoners comfortable but stories of inhuman treatment at his hands spread in the North. This was partly because of crowded conditions on the *Alabama*, and partly because he kept some of the prisoners in irons to retaliate for the treatment of former paymaster Henry Myers of the *Sumter*. Myers and former U.S. Consul T.T. Tunstall, who had opted for the Confederacy, had been arrested at Tangier at the request of the U.S. consul. After being held in irons in prison there they were transferred to a U.S. merchant ship, the captain of which ordered their heads shaved. He also kept the two men in irons for the duration of the passage to the United States.

Although unquestionably the ablest of the Confederate raider captains and a man who for the most part treated his captives with respect and dignity, Semmes was also a maverick who never did get on particularly well with either his superiors or his subordinates. He seems to have been an excellent captain who paid attention to detail and was a stickler for order and cleanliness in the ship (none of his crew ever died of disease). He was also a staunch Catholic. Semmes also seems to have been an opinionated, wordy individual given to hyperbole. Proud and entirely self-satisfied, he never seemed to see any wrong with his own cause and only evil and unfairness on the part of his adversaries. His memoirs reveal a lot about him and show the great bitterness he felt toward the North and his contempt for the U.S. Navy. Semmes's imperial style, martial bearing, chin whiskers, and long waxed mustaches that ended in fine waxed points led his sailors to refer to him as "Old Beeswax," "Old Bim," or "Marshal Pomp."

The vast majority of the *Alabama*'s crew were British. They had been recruited among the castoffs of Liverpool and Semmes noted on August 1, 1863, "I have a precious set of rascals on board, faithless in the matter of abiding by their contracts, liars, thieves and drunkards." Porter said of them, "It was not a crew of enthusiastic Southerners who were going forth to fight for a cause they really loved, but a band of foreign mercenaries who had no feeling but of indifference towards either of the combatants; and when one thinks of the character of these sailors there is some excuse for comparing them to pirates who fight with no motive than that of plunder."

In November 1862, however, Semmes expressed himself well pleased with his men, noting in his journal on the sixteenth: "I have never seen a better disposed or more orderly crew. They have come very kindly into the traces." Semmes continued to have problems with crew conduct, however, especially on the infrequent occasions when the *Alabama* was in port.

Certainly the *Alabama*'s crew was a reckless and hard-drinking lot. After taking the first prize vessel Semmes read them the Confederate "Articles of War" and told them they were bound by them. He tried as much as possible to keep them under tight discipline and seldom allowed them ashore, but he never did succeed in welding the polyglot group of many nationalities into a smooth-working team. Only half of the crew remained with the ship during her nearly two years of existence. There were deaths, desertions, and injuries, but Semmes was never short of men; enough volunteered along the way from among crews of his prizes to keep the crew at normal complement.

If his crew was perhaps indifferent, Semmes's officers were quite capable. The first three lieutenants had served with him on the *Sumter*. The most important of these was certainly First Lieutenant John McIntosh Kell, who again served as his execu-

John McIntosh Kell: born Georgia 1823, the son of John and Margery (Baillie) Kell; entered the U.S. Navy as a midshipman in 1841; passed midshipman 1847; during the Mexican War he served in vessels along the California Coast; he partici- pated in the expedition sent to Paraguay against Lopez and also was part of Perry's expedition to Japan; court-martialed for disobeying an order he considered illegal, his defense attorney was Raphael Semmes; Kell was convicted and dis- missed from the service, but reinstated in 1850; five years later, he was promoted to master and then to lieutenant; married Julia Blanche Munroe in 1856; they had six children; resigned from the U.S. Navy in 1861 to accept a Confederate appointment; served as executive officer under Raphael Semmes on the *Sumter* and on the *Alabama*; promoted to full captain late in the war, Kell commanded the ironclad *Richmond* on the James River; there is no record of his surrendering; finding himself poverty stricken after the war, he settled in Sunnyside, Georgia, and engaged in farming; he declined to take part in Georgia politics, yet he nevertheless served as the state's adjutant general from 1886 to 1900; his *Recollections of a Naval Life* appeared in 1900, the year he died in Sunnyside.

Some of the officers who served on the *Alabama. Top, left to right*: Irvine
Bulloch, Arthur Sinclair, Eugene Maffit. *Center:* Richard Armstrong.
Bottom, left to right: Beckett Howell, G.T. Fullam, L.R. Anderson.

tive officer. Kell oversaw the operation of the ship and dealt with her crew; he later wrote a book about his experiences. The other two lieutenants were Richard F. Armstrong and Joseph D. Wilson. Also from the *Sumter* came Surgeon Francis L. Galt, Lieutenant Beckett K. Howell of the Marines, and Chief Engineer Miles J. Freeman. Arthur F. Sinclair, whose father and grandfather had both been U.S. Navy officers, was fourth lieutenant. He, too, wrote a book about his time on the *Alabama*. Lieutenant B. K. Howell was President Davis's brother-in-law. Acting Master Irvine S. Bulloch was the younger half-brother of Confederate agent James Bulloch, and Midshipman Eugene A. Maffit was the son of the *Florida*'s captain. Semmes recruited British subject Dr. David Llewellyn as assistant surgeon.

In two weeks Semmes had decimated the Union whaling fleet in the Azores, but bad weather was upon him. On September 18 when the crew fired the whaler *Elisha Dunbar* a gale was already blowing. Semmes remembered it this way:

> This burning ship was a beautiful spectacle, the scenes being wild and picturesque beyond description....The thunder began to roll, and crash, and the lightning to leap from cloud to cloud in a thousand eccentric lines. The sea was in a tumult of rage, the winds howled, and floods of rain descended. Amid the turmoil of the elements, the *Dunbar*, all in flames, and with disordered gear and unfurled canvas, lay rolling and tossing upon the sea. Now an ignited sail would fly from a yard, and scud off before the gale; and now the yard itself, released from the control of its braces, would swing about wildly, as in the madness of despair, and then drop into the sea. Finally the masts went by the board, and then the hull rocked to and fro for a while, until it was filled with water, and the fire nearly quenched, when it set-

tled to the bottom of the great deep, a victim to the passions of man and the fury of the elements.

The *Alabama* herself came through the storm unscathed. Her decks leaked from want of caulking, however, making life miserable for the prisoners below. Semmes then sailed his ship west to waters off Newfoundland and New England—the sea lanes where many Union vessels laden with Midwestern grain for Europe would pass. Ships that the *Alabama* took off the Newfoundland Banks tended to be large and with valuable cargoes. Ironically, destroying vessels laden with wheat for Britain and France was not in Confederate interests. Britain was a net importer of food and "King Corn" was actually more important to political stability in the British Isles than "King Cotton." Driving up grain prices at a time when there was a European wheat shortage reminded London and Paris of the importance of good relations with the North. In twenty-six days in October Semmes took eleven vessels, destroying eight of these and letting the other three go on bond.

On October 9 Semmes took the *Tonawanda*. Bound from Philadelphia to Liverpool, she had sixty women and children on board. As Semmes noted, "The men we might have disposed of, without much inconvenience, but it was not possible to convert the *Alabama* into a nursery and set the stewards to serving pap to the babies. Although I made it a rule never to bond a ship if I could burn her, I released the *Tonawanda* on bond, though there was no legal impediment to her being burned." In fact, the *Tonawanda* was made to follow after the *Alabama* for several days, Semmes hoping to find another ship in which he could deposit her passengers and thus be able to burn her. When, two days later, he took the *Manchester*, also bound for Liverpool, she turned out to have a more valuable cargo so he burned her and let the *Tonawanda* go on an $80,000 bond with her passengers, as well as those of the latest capture and the *Wave Crest* and *Dunkirk*.

Semmes kept two men from the latest captures aboard the *Alabama*. The first, from the *Dunkirk*, had been a seaman on the *Sumter* who had deserted at Cádiz. He now found himself forced to serve on the *Alabama* for the duration of her cruise without pay or prize money. Later court-martialed for drunkenness, he was left as punishment on Blanquilla Island off Venezuela.

Semmes also kept one of the passengers from the *Tonawanda*, an African American named David White. Semmes noted:

> This was a likely negro lad of about seventeen years of age—a slave until he was twenty-one, under the laws of Delaware. This little State, all of whose sympathies were with us, had been ridden over, rough-shod, by the Vandals north of her, as Maryland afterward was, and was arrayed on the side of the enemy. I was obliged, therefore, to treat her as such. The slave was on his way to Europe, in company with his master. He came necessarily under the laws of war, and I brought him on board the *Alabama*, where we were in want of good servants, and sent him to wait on the ward-room mess.

In his memoirs Semmes noted the "howl" raised in the North over his "capture," but how happy "Dave" really was in his new surroundings (when serving Dr. Galt, Semmes wrote, his "ivories" would shine) and on leave ashore. Semmes said he had "caused his name to be entered on the books of the ship, as one of the crew, and allowed him the pay of his grade." Northerners, Semmes asserted, "know as little about the negro and his nature as they do about the people of the South."

It was not the U.S. Navy but nature that interrupted the *Alabama*'s activities. A hurricane came up from the south and commerce raiding was forgotten as the crew of the *Alabama*

Gideon Welles: born Connecticut 1802; he attended the Episcopal Academy at Cheshire, Connecticut, and the American Literary, Scientific, and Military Academy at Norwich, Vermont; he also studied law, but embarked on a career in journalism; in 1826 he became an owner and the editor of the *Hartford Times*; that year he won election to the Connecticut legislature, where he served until 1835; he fought against debt-related imprisonment, religious- and property-based voting requirements, and authored the state's first general incorporation laws; he supported individual freedom, strict construction of the Constitution, and states' rights; elected three times to the state office of comptroller of public accounts, he was appointed postmaster of Hartford 1836; in 1846 he began a four-year stint as chief of the Navy's Bureau of Provisions and Clothing; in 1850 he failed to win election to the U.S. Senate; a long-time Democrat he joined the Republicans, chiefly over the slavery issue; in 1856 he helped establish the pro-Republican *Hartford Evening Press*, and became a frequent contributor; also that year he lost a bid to become governor of Connecticut; in 1860 president-elect Abraham Lincoln selected Welles for his cabinet; in March 1861 he became secretary of the navy and took on the daunting job of building and modernizing a naval force during a time of war; in this he was quite successful; he oversaw massive ship-building projects, the development of ironclad vessels, and important advances in armaments and ordnance; his was among the government's most efficiently run departments; he was also a strong moderating

influence within Lincoln's cabinet; although fiercely loyal to the president, he opposed Lincoln's excessive uses of power, such as the suppression of the press and the suspension of *Habeas Corpus*; he vigorously supported Lincoln's moderate approach to restoring Southern states to the Union and, after Lincoln's assassination, provided the same support for President Andrew Johnson, steadfastly backing him during the impeachment proceedings; after his retirement in 1869, Welles wrote several articles and published a book, *Lincoln and Seward*, in 1874; Welles died in 1878; he was one of only two cabinet members to serve throughout Lincoln's administration; the *Diary of Gideon Welles,* published posthumously in three volumes, remains among the most important historical sources from that period.

fought to save their ship. While tossed about by the violent storm, which reached its height on October 16—sails were split and the main yard snapped—the *Alabama* succeeded in passing through it. Throughout her career she proved to be an excellent ship in heavy weather.

By this time the Northern press and shipowners were demanding action to find and destroy the *Alabama* and other Confederate cruisers. Although U.S. Secretary of the Navy Gideon Welles, supported by President Lincoln, assigned top priority to the naval blockade of the Confederacy, more than a dozen Union warships were already searching for the *Alabama*. They were always a little late or their captains looked for her in the wrong location. Why the major shipping lane between New England and Europe was not better protected is something of a mystery. As Porter noted, the U.S. Navy was increasingly successful in blockading Confederate ports but was never very effective in protecting its own merchant marine.

Semmes then sailed the *Alabama* to the Caribbean to meet the tender *Agrippina*, which acted as his coaler. On November 16 the crew sighted the island of Dominica, the first land made since leaving the Azores. Semmes now put the *Alabama* under steam and ran for Martinique to the harbor of Fort de France, where she anchored on November 18. There he landed prisoners and took on provisions. The *Agrippina* had arrived a week earlier.

Boats that came out to the *Alabama* brought not only tobacco and fresh fruit for the crew but also hard liquor, which was then smuggled on board. Many of the men proceeded to get drunk and some threatened mutiny. Semmes wrote later that he quickly saw that it was "a drunken mutiny...and not very alarming." When Kell had gone forward to quell the disturbance, a sailor had thrown a belaying-pin at him and others had verbally abused him and threatened "personal violence." Semmes ordered the crew beat to quarters. Once his officers were all armed Semmes then reviewed the men, picked out those who were drunk, and had them arrested and clapped in irons. He then had the quartermasters rapidly douse the worst offenders with buckets of seawater as they gasped for breath until they were sober. It was, as Semmes noted with satisfaction, "my first, and only mutiny on board the *Alabama*."

This was a minor problem next to the situation that arose the next morning. Apprehensive over the possible appearance of a U.S. Navy warship searching for him, Semmes did not attempt to coal the *Alabama* at Fort de France. Instead he ordered his coaler to Blanquilla Island off the Venezuelan coast. This precaution was a wise one for the tender was hardly clear of the harbor when the more heavily armed U.S. Navy screw frigate *San Jacinto* (Commander William Ronckendorff) arrived. Ronckendorff identified the *Alabama* and positioned his ship to blockade the harbor. Armed with one 100-pounder rifled gun, ten IX-inch Dahlgren smoothbores, and one 20-pounder rifled gun, the *San Jacinto* had double the Confederate raider's armament and crew.

All day the *Alabama*'s crew watched their counterparts prepare for battle. They need not have worried. Although heavily armed, the Union frigate was old and slow (only seven knots under steam). Ronckendorff devised an alarm system of signals by rocket from boats and an American brig in the harbor, but that night Semmes took advantage of a rain squall to leave with lights out and all guns manned. He then sailed to Blanquilla to rendezvous with the *Agrippina* and recoal, which took several days.

6

THE *ALABAMA* AND THE *HATTERAS*

Semmes then departed from his mission to destroy Union commercial shipping. Newspapers from a British ship brought news that Union forces had taken Galveston, Texas, and that a Union expeditionary force under General Nathaniel Banks was expected to invade the state in January. Semmes knew Galveston harbor was shallow and that Union transports would have to anchor offshore, and he hoped to swoop down on and destroy a number of them. On the way to Galveston he planned to intercept steamers from Panama. In those days before the Panama Canal, travelers to California went by steamer from New York to Aspinwall (now Colón) and then by rail across the Isthmus of Panama where they caught another steamer to San Francisco. Semmes hoped to catch at least one such ship traveling northward with gold.

On November 29 the *Alabama* stood for the Mona Passage between San Domingo and Puerto Rico, the usual route for mail steamers on their way north. He took several ships there, and on December 7 overhauled the large bark-rigged steamer *Ariel* of the Aspinwall Line. The captain of the *Ariel* tried to outrun the *Alabama*, and Semmes had two shots fired at her, one of which struck the *Ariel's* foremast. Her captain decided discretion was the better part of valor and ordered her stopped and her flag lowered. The *Ariel* was a third larger than the *Alabama*, but Semmes was disappointed to discover that she was outward bound rather than returning from California with a rich cargo. Nonetheless, she was probably the *Alabama's* most important prize. She had on board more than 700 people, including some 500 passengers (half of them women and children) and a battalion of U.S. Marines (140 men) on their way to Pacific Squadron assignments. Semmes disarmed the Marines and paroled them.

Semmes had the *Ariel* sail in company and it was not until he had given up on falling in with another merchantman on which he could place her passengers that he was obliged to let her go under bond, her skipper promising to pay $216,000 to the Confederate States of America. It was a big disappointment to Semmes that he could not burn the *Ariel*, especially as she was owned by Cornelius Vanderbilt. He knew that Vanderbilt had given a fast steamer (the *Vanderbilt*) to the U.S. Government for the express purpose of hunting down Confederate commerce raiders such as the *Alabama*. Also to his chagrin he learned that the next northbound packet was to be the *Ariel* herself; when she did indeed make that next trip it was without gold.

Semmes then took the *Alabama* into the Gulf of Mexico. On December 23, 1862, he rendezvoused with the *Agrippina* at the Arcas Islands off the coast of Yucatán. The crew spent the next week taking on supplies and coal, and Semmes gave them shore leave on the uninhabited coral islands.

Semmes and his crew then prepared for the raid on the Banks expedition, expected at Galveston in early January. His plan was to arrive at Galveston during daylight, take careful note of the disposition of transports, and then return for a night attack when he could inflict the maximum damage and confusion. The plan appeared to have a good chance of success as the *Alabama* was faster than U.S. Navy blockaders along the coast and could thus run or fight on her choosing.

On January 5 the *Alabama* left the Arcas Islands for Galveston, arriving off that port in the late afternoon of the eleventh. Semmes did not know that Galveston had been retaken on the first. The Banks expedition had been diverted to New Orleans and instead of a fleet of Federal transports, the *Alabama*'s lookouts saw only five Union blockading warships lobbing shells into the port city.

Semmes had taken his ship in too close and Union seamen also sighted the *Alabama*, although they could not identify her. Suspicions were aroused, however, when the *Alabama* stopped some twelve miles offshore. Union squadron commander Commodore Henry H. Bell flew his flag in the twenty-one-gun steam sloop *Brooklyn*, the same ship that had unsuccessfully chased the *Sumter* in her escape from New Orleans. Bell did not have his flagship available; she was immobilized by a non-functioning steam engine and so he sent the *Hatteras* (Lieutenant-Commander Homer C. Blake) to investigate. She was a former Delaware River excursion side-wheel steamer and only lightly armed: four light 32-pounders (27cwt) and one 20-pounder rifle. Although the *Hatteras* was a poor match for the *Alabama* this did not stop Semmes from maintaining that the battle was an equal one: the *Hatteras* was a heavier ship with a large crew (108 on the *Hatteras* to 110 on the *Alabama*), and, Semmes claimed, just as many guns; he gave the *Hatteras* two additional rifled 30-pounder guns and a 12-pounder howitzer, making eight in all.

Semmes, who had promised his crew some excitement at

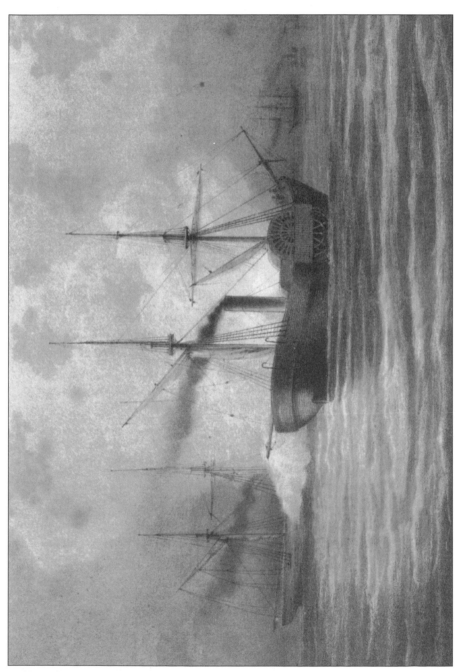

Combat between the *Alabama* and the *Hatteras*

Galveston, was undecided as to what to do next and so was relieved to see the *Hatteras* put out. Under topsails only, the *Alabama* moved slowly along the coast, drawing the Union warship away from the protection of the other blockaders. As soon as it was dark and when they were about twenty miles from the Federal squadron, the *Alabama* lay to and then turned toward the *Hatteras* under steam. The two ships were within hailing distance when Blake demanded his opponent's identity. In what Porter called "pure perfidy, such as a Zulu warrior would resort to," Semmes identified his ship as Her Britannic Majesty's steamer *Petrel* (some accounts say *Ariel*). Reassured, Blake demanded the right to inspect the ship's registry in accordance with international law. After a boat had been lowered and was underway from the *Hatteras*, Semmes called out, "This is the Confederate States steamer *Alabama*. Fire." The first broadside from the *Alabama* was decisive, the *Hatteras* staggering under its force.

The battle took place at very short range and both crews fired small arms as well as their main guns. Blake knew the weakness of his ship and tried to ram his opponent. But the *Hatteras* was too slow and the *Alabama* easily avoided her. The battle was soon over; shots from the *Alabama* set the *Hatteras* on fire and smashed into her steam engine, immobilizing her. Within thirteen minutes, with two of his seamen dead, five others wounded, his ship sinking, and the *Alabama* in position to rake her, Blake surrendered. The *Alabama* had only two men wounded. She had taken only five shells from the *Hatteras*, one of which had failed to explode. The remainder of the *Hatteras*'s crew were then taken on board and the *Alabama* speedily departed without lights. The *Hatteras* was the only U.S. Navy warship sunk by a Confederate raider during the war. On January 20 the *Alabama* arrived at Port Royal, Jamaica, where Semmes paroled his prisoners. The *Hatteras*'s boat crew escaped, the men rowing back to the Union fleet to report what had happened.

7
THE *ALABAMA* RESUMES HER HUNT FOR PRIZES

The *Alabama* remained in the West Indies for the next month. When she was in port a number of British naval officers paid courtesy calls on the ship and the British governor allowed Semmes to recoal. In his discussion of the *Alabama*'s career Porter wrote scathingly, with some justification, of the friendly treatment British authorities extended to the crew of the *Alabama* and the opposite treatment meted out to U.S. Navy officers and men.

On January 25 the *Alabama* left Jamaica to sail east through the West Indies to Brazil. Soon after her departure the *Alabama* took as prize the *Golden Rule*, bound to Aspinwall, Panama, from New York. Her cargo included spars, sails, masts, and rigging for the U.S.S. *Bainbridge*, which had been laid up at Aspinwall after a bad storm. She was burned near San Domingo. Semmes described the scene:

A looker-on upon that conflagration would have seen a wonderful picture, for besides the burning ship, there were the two islands mentioned [St. Domingo and Jamaica], sleeping in the dreamy moonlight on a calm bosom of a tropical sea, and the rakish-looking "British pirate" steaming in for the land, with every spar and line of cordage brought out in bold relief by the bright flame—nay, with the very "pirates" themselves visible, handling the boxes and bales of merchandise which they had "robbed" from this innocent Yankee, whose countrymen at home were engaged in the Christian occupation of burning our houses and desolating our fields.

In the first three months of 1863 the *Alabama* took thirteen prizes, in addition to sinking the *Hatteras*. Finally, on April 4 the *Alabama* overtook the *Louisa Hatch* carrying coal from Cardiff to Ceylon and claimed as French. Semmes concluded that documentation was lacking to support the claim. His own ship was low on coal so Semmes ordered the *Louisa Hatch* to accompany the *Alabama*. The coal was transferred beginning on the night of April 10 off the Brazilian island of Fernando de Noronha. Later Semmes ordered the *Louisa Hatch* burned. The decision to transfer coal from the prize to the *Alabama* was fortuitous, as there was no sign of the *Agrippina*, which had been delayed. On April 22 Semmes took the *Alabama* back out to sea and headed for Bahia. He captured several prizes en route and reached there on the eleventh. Two days later the C.S.S. *Georgia* came in and, at the time, the C.S.S. *Florida* was only a hundred miles to the north. The only Union warship in the South Atlantic was the screw sloop *Mohican*, sister ship to the *Kearsarge*. Acting Rear Admiral Charles Wilkes, commander of the West Indian Squadron (created specifically to track down the *Alabama* and *Florida*), had detained in the West Indies as his flagship the powerful, fast steamer *Vanderbilt*

(Acting Lieutenant C.H. Baldwin: two 100-pounder rifled guns, twelve IX-inch Dahlgren smoothbores, and one 12-pounder rifle), which should have been operating with the *Mohican*. The *Mohican* herself only missed the Confederate cruisers in several locations by a few days. Wilkes seemed more interested in capturing blockade runners for their prize money than hunting the *Alabama*. Later, Secretary of the Navy Welles relieved him of command of the West Indian Squadron for "wholly inexcusable" misconduct in holding the *Vanderbilt*.

On May 21, 1863, fully coaled, the *Alabama* sailed from Bahia. She then cruised off the Brazilian coast between Bahia and Rio de Janeiro. The *Agrippina* did not arrive at Bahia until June 1, only to discover two U.S. Navy warships in port—the *Mohican* and the sailing schooner *Onward*. Captain Alexander McQueen of the *Agrippina* tried to figure out a way to deliver his coal but was fearful his ship and its contents might be seized by the Federal vessels when he left port. On the advice of the British consul, he sold the coal and took cargo for Britain. The *Agrippina* never did encounter the *Alabama* again.

Between Bahia and Rio the *Alabama* took eight prizes, five of which were burned and two bonded. The remaining prize was the 500-ton bark *Conrad*, taken on June 20. Sinclair wrote of her, "A more beautiful specimen of American clipper could not be produced,—new, well-found, and fast, and, being barque-rigged, easy to handle with a small crew." Semmes made her an auxiliary cruiser and commissioned her the *Tuscaloosa*, noting, "It was meet that a child of the *Alabama* should be named after one of the towns of the State." She was armed with two bronze 12-pounders on ship carriages (gun mounts)—part of the cargo of the *Talisman* bound for China, a prize taken two weeks before. Semmes made Lieutenant John Low her captain; Midshipman William Sinclair was first lieutenant under an acting commission from Semmes. A dozen men from the *Alabama* made up her crew.

In three months off Latin America Semmes had taken fifteen prizes, and during this period he had never spotted a U.S. Navy warship. Porter wrote:

> It had never occurred to the American Government to send half-a-dozen gunboats or 'double-enders' to these latitudes. They could have easily been spared, and a depot for coaling vessels could have been established under the smooth waters of the equator, at which all the vessels-of-war of the Navy could have been supplied. If the *Alabama* knew where to go to catch American merchantmen, why did not the Federal Government know where to seek the *Alabama*? . . . It was not the particular smartness of Semmes that enabled him to escape capture. It was the omission or indifference of the Navy Department in not sending proper vessels to the right localities.

But it was time to find new hunting ground, and Semmes ordered the *Tuscaloosa* to proceed on her own and rendezvous with him at Cape Town. Low subsequently captured two merchantmen valued at $310,000. When the *Tuscaloosa* arrived at Cape Town the question for British authorities was whether she was a legal warship. Ultimately they determined she was not and seized her on December 26, 1863.

Among the ships the *Alabama* soon overhauled were several former U.S. merchantmen now legally registered in foreign countries—evidence of the effect Confederate cruisers were having on Union trade. Semmes now sailed the *Alabama* to the vicinity of the Cape of Good Hope where he could intercept vessels homeward bound from the East Indies.

On the night of July 2, during the passage to Africa, Semmes chased and almost exchanged shots with a large ship that turned out to be H.M.S. *Diomede*. On July 28 the *Alabama* anchored in Saldanha Bay, about seventy-five miles northwest of Cape Town. After ascertaining that there were no U.S. Navy warships in the vicinity, Semmes ordered maintenance work performed on the ship. On August 5, after accomplishing this, she left for Cape Town. That same day she encountered the *Tuscaloosa* on her way to Simon's Bay to refit. Also that day the *Alabama* took as a prize the bark *Sea Bride*. There was some question about the exact location of the prize during her capture. Semmes claimed that when she was taken the *Sea Bride* was five to six miles offshore, well beyond the three-mile territorial limit. The American consul, however, protested what he claimed was a violation of British sovereignty. After investigation British authorities allowed Semmes to keep the prize. Semmes had the *Sea Bride* sailed up the west coast beyond British jurisdiction to Angra Pequenha, where he sold her to a less than scrupulous buyer from Cape Town for $16,940. This was less than a third of her estimated value, but the buyer was taking some risk since Semmes did not have legal papers for the transfer.

Hundreds of people at Cape Town came to see the *Alabama* while she was there, and others visited her at the more protected anchorage of Simon's Bay where Semmes moved her on August 9. On August 12 British photographers came aboard to take pictures. These photographs were then transformed into wood engravings and printed in England.

On August 15, a day after learning of the Battle of Gettysburg, Semmes again took the *Alabama* to sea. By now weariness had set in. Semmes recorded in his journal, "How tiresome is the routine of cruising becoming." On returning to Cape Town he heard the further discouraging news of the fall of Vicksburg and Port Hudson.

After the sale of the *Sea Bride* the *Tuscaloosa* and the *Alabama* separated. Semmes ordered Low to cruise off Brazil, with the two ships to rendezvous later. In two months off South Africa the *Alabama* had achieved only the negligible result of one ship taken. More importantly, Semmes learned that the U.S. Navy steamer *Vanderbilt* (Acting Lieutenant C.H. Baldwin) was in the vicinity searching for him. The *Vanderbilt* was both larger and faster than the *Alabama*. She had arrived at Cape Town on August 30, but Baldwin had intended to get

Lieutenants Sinclair and Armstrong on deck of the *Alabama*

there earlier and, had he done so, the *Vanderbilt* would certainly have caught the *Alabama* at Cape Town. The Union warship had been delayed by coaling problems and because her boilers were so corroded that they had to be scaled. The two ships played a game of cat and mouse for about a week. Time was running out for the *Alabama*.

The year 1863 was in fact the high point for Confederate commerce destroyers. The *Alabama* took only three prizes in the first six months of 1864. President Lincoln and his advisers had been loath to weaken the blockade by detaching cruisers to look for commerce raiders, but the growth of the U.S. Navy from 427 vessels in December 1862 to 588 a year later allowed the dispatch of some vessels to areas where they might encounter the Confederate raiders and put an end to their depredations.

Semmes now decided to take the *Alabama* into the Pacific. On September 24 she left Cape Town to sail through the Indian Ocean into the China Sea—by a roundabout route that took his ship far to the south of the island of Mauritius so as to avoid the *Vanderbilt*. Unknown to Semmes, however, a two-foot crack in the starboard paddle wheel shaft forced the *Vanderbilt* to give up the chase and return home. Thus the chief event of the *Alabama*'s nineteen-day trip across the Indian Ocean was on October 16, when the *Alabama* encountered a bad storm that smashed one of her boats. It was the anniversary of the hurricane a year before. After the storm passed Semmes put the crew to work painting and cleaning the battered ship.

Semmes had high expectations for his voyage to the East Indies, hoping he could make serious inroads into the U.S. merchantmen engaged in the Orient trade. In Sundra Strait Between November 6 and 11 the *Alabama* took three merchantmen and burned them. Another fell to him on the sixteenth. By now, however, Semmes was having troubles with his crew. His own diary entries reflect the situation noted by the chief officer of the *Contest* (taken on November 11), made while he was aboard the *Alabama* as a prisoner: "Crew much dissatisfied, no prize money, no liberty, and see no prospect of getting any. Discipline very slack; steamer dirty, rigging slovenly. Semmes sometimes punishes but is afraid to push too hard; men excited; officers do not report to captain; crew do things for which they would be shot on board American man-of-war."

The captain of the *Contest* had seen to it that she lived up to her name. When the *Alabama* ran down her false U.S. flag and replaced it with her true Confederate one, he ordered sails put on and ignored a Confederate shot that fell short. After a lengthy chase the *Alabama* was able to draw close enough to fire another shot, this one between the *Contest*'s masts. This time her captain ordered her hove to. "We had never captured so beautiful a vessel," Sinclair wrote. "She was a revelation of symmetry, a very race horse. A sacrilege, almost a desecration, to destroy so perfect a specimen of man's handiwork." Nonetheless, after ordering her useful stores removed, Semmes had the *Contest* burned.

To overtake the *Contest* the *Alabama* had been pressed to her limits of steam and sail. By now it was apparent the ship was wearing out. Her hull copper plating was coming loose and her boilers were so corroded that it was dangerous to use full steam. The uncertainty and strain were showing on all, Semmes included. Lieutenant Sinclair noted, "He must have a rugged constitution and iron nerves to pull through as he does. At all hours of the day and night he may be seen bent over his chart in the cabin, or on deck conning the surroundings. A heavy responsibility...."

On December 3 the *Alabama* made land at the French island group of Puolo Condore. Semmes then tried the Malacca Strait. On December 21 the *Alabama* arrived at Singapore. Rumors of the ship's presence had evidently preceded her and at Singapore Semmes found twenty-two U.S. merchant ships safely laid up in the harbor. He heard of others secure at Bangkok, Canton, Shanghai, and Manila. At almost every port she touched some men deserted; at Singapore twelve men left the ship but another six signed on. From neutral ships Semmes learned that the screw sloop *Wyoming*, a bark-rigged Federal gunboat (two IX-inch Dahlgrens in pivot and four 32-pounders in broadsides), the sole U.S. Navy warship on the China station, was patrolling Sunda Strait between Sumatra and Java. As the *Alabama* was somewhat more powerful Semmes resolved to attack the *Wyoming*, but Semmes discovered she was no longer on station there. The *Wyoming*'s captain, Commander David M. McDougal, had learned of the presence of the *Alabama* on November 22, and, at one point the two ships had been only twenty-five miles apart as McDougal searched for Semmes without result. But McDougal believed Semmes would continue into the China Sea and so he sailed from Singapore for Manila—the opposite direction from his adversary, who left Singapore on December 24 and almost immediately took as prize the bark *Martaban* (formerly the *Texas Star*). Her captain claimed British registry but Semmes burned her. British Vice Admiral Sir James Hope then issued an order that could have sent the Royal Navy in chase of the *Alabama*. It required British warships to "capture and send to England for adjudication in the admiralty court every vessel by which a British vessel is burned at sea." A footnote exempted the *Alabama* in this instance by noting that the *Martaban* was a doubtful case. Semmes said the *Martaban*'s captain later gave a deposition that he had falsified the registry to avoid capture. Although the *Martaban* was ultimately ruled by an international claims commission to have been an American vessel and thus a legal capture, Semmes's refusal to recognize British authority in this instance alienated British insurers and shippers from the Confederate cause.

The *Alabama* then sailed through the Straits of Malacca and the day after Christmas took two more U.S. merchant

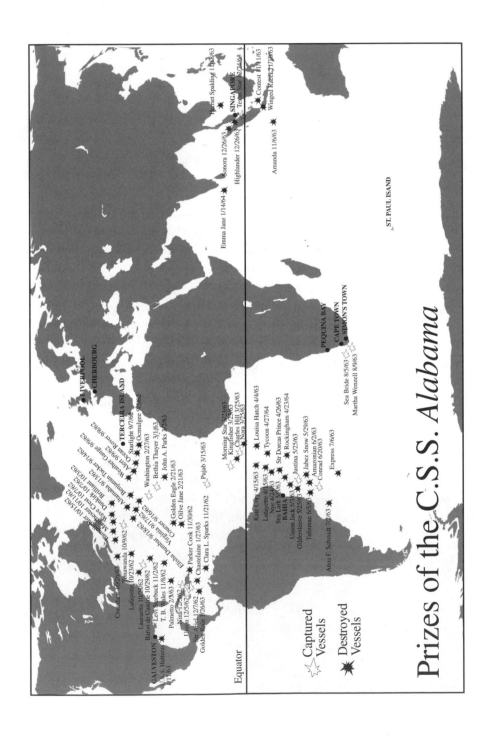

Prizes of the C.S.S. *Alabama*

ships, bringing the year's total to thirty-seven. But now the morale of the crew was very low. Semmes had already decided to seek a modern shipyard in Britain or France to carry out a complete overhaul of his vessel.

On December 31 the *Alabama* reentered the Indian Ocean. In the Bay of Bengal, she made a brief call at Anjenga on the southwestern Indian coast, where Semmes landed prisoners. She then sailed west to the Comoro Islands near the coast of Africa to reprovision. Since Islam was the religion there and thus there would be no legal sale of alcohol, Semmes gave his men shore leave. Four men deserted but were soon returned to the ship.

On February 12 the *Alabama* left the Comoros, retracing her course back through the Indian Ocean to Cape Town, where she arrived on March 20. On the return trip Semmes took only one vessel. While at Cape Town he learned that the British had seized the *Tuscaloosa* on December 26 when she entered port for repair. Semmes protested to the British admiral who had carried out the seizure. Actually the local governor, who thought it unjustified, had already initiated correspondence with London regarding the matter. Eventually the *Tuscaloosa* was turned over to the American consul.

Although the fortunes of war were forcing a change in the British attitude toward the Confederacy, the *Alabama* remained as popular as ever. Crowds of people came to see and tour the famous ship. By now, however, the *Alabama* had been in commission for almost twenty months. Her bottom was foul and her machinery in poor repair. Semmes noted, "Many of the beams of the ship are splitting and giving way, owing to the greenness of the timber of which she was built." It was time to return to Europe, even though this meant a sizable risk of encountering Union warships there.

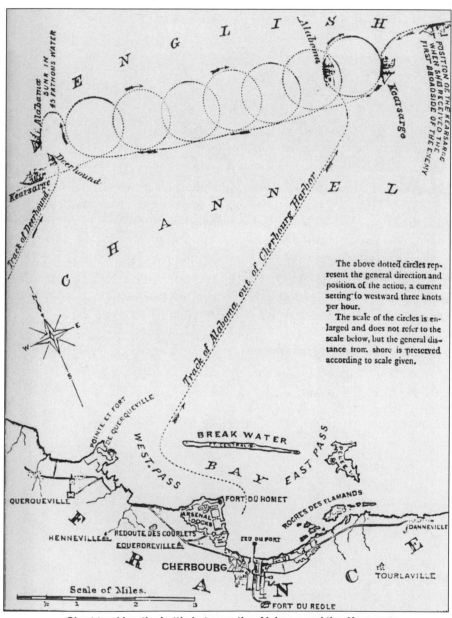

The above dotted circles represent the general direction and position of the action, a current setting to westward three knots per hour.

The scale of the circles is enlarged and does not refer to the scale below, but the general distance from shore is preserved according to scale given.

Chart tracking the battle between the *Alabama* and the *Kearsarge*

8

THE *ALABAMA* AND
THE *KEARSARGE*

On March 25 the *Alabama* left Cape Town for Europe. As she sailed out she met coming in the U.S. merchantman *Quang Tung* on her way to China. If Semmes had sailed a bit earlier he would have caught her in international waters. On her way to Europe the *Alabama* took two more prizes—as it turned out, her last. Semmes had both ships burned; the *Rockingham*, with a cargo of guano, on April 23, and the fine clipper ship *Tycoon*, with general cargo, on the twenty-eighth. Although he stopped other ships and examined their papers, Semmes had to let all of them go.

Before burning the *Rockingham*, Semmes used the abandoned ship for target practice. Semmes noted in his journal for April 23 "reasonable success" for the practice firing, and in his memoirs Lieutenant Sinclair recorded "considerable damage" to the target in "fine execution." But the practice revealed an ominous fact: the black powder had lost some of its force in projecting shot. Extremes of temperature and dampness had accelerated normal deterioration that would have occurred from long storage. Caps and fuses were also defective, with only one shell in three exploding. Semmes had new fuses installed on all the shells aboard ship, and defective powder stored in barrels was thrown overboard. Semmes thought that the powder made up in cartridges and kept in sealed copper canisters was satisfactory; only after the engagement with the *Kearsarge* did he conclude that it, too, was not at full strength and might have lost a third of its power.

As his ship sailed north Semmes wrote in his journal on May 21: "Fired a blank cartridge at a ship which overhauled and passed us. She showed English colors. Our bottom is in such a state that everything passes us. We are like a crippled hunter limping home from a long chase." In his memoirs he was more poetic and stressed the toll of the voyage on himself:

> She was like the wearied fox-hound, limping back after a long chase, foot-sore, and longing for quiet and repose. Her commander, like herself, was well-nigh worn down. Vigils by night and by day, the storm and the drenching rain, the frequent and rapid change of climate, now freezing, now melting or boiling, and the constant excitement of the chase and capture, had laid, in the three years of war he had been afloat, a load of a dozen years on his shoulders. The shadows of a sorrowful future, too, began to rest upon his spirit.

On June 10, 1864, the *Alabama* reached Cap de la Hague on the Normandy coast, picked up a pilot, and the next day dropped anchor at Cherbourg. Since her commissioning she had sailed the incredible distance of 75,000 miles, taken sixty-six prizes, and sunk a Union warship worth $160,000. In the *Sumter* and the *Alabama* together Semmes had taken a total of eighty-four Union merchantmen. Semmes estimated he had burned $4,613,914 worth of shipping and cargoes and bonded others valued at $562,250. Another estimate places the total at nearly $6 million. Twenty-five Union warships had been engaged in searching for the *Alabama*, costing the federal government over $7 million. Beyond this financial toll, her exploits had been a considerable boost to Confederate morale.

Immediately on his arrival Semmes requested permission to land his prisoners and to put the *Alabama* into dry dock for repair. French Government officials refused the latter, pointing out, as Semmes knew, that the facilities at Cherbourg were reserved for ships of the French Navy. Permission to use them could be granted only by Emperor Napoleon III, who was away from Paris. The authorities recommended that he move his ship to Le Havre or some other port with private dockyard facilities. Semmes was confident that eventually the French government, which supported the Confederate cause and had a vested interest (its own Mexican venture) in its victory, would grant him permission. The emperor did decide to relax the one-day rule regarding the presence of a belligerent in the French port, and Semmes promptly sent thirty-eight prisoners from his last two captures ashore and granted his men leave.

News of the *Alabama*'s arrival spread quickly and people flocked to Cherbourg to see the famous raider. On June 12 U.S. Minister Dayton in Paris telegraphed news of the Confederate ship's arrival to the Dutch port of Flushing where the Union third-rate screw steam sloop *Kearsarge*, Captain John A. Winslow, was riding at anchor. She was on station in the channel to monitor the *Georgia* and *Rappahannock* at Calais and also watch for Confederate vessels under construction in French yards. Dayton cautioned Winslow to avoid hostilities with the *Alabama* in French territorial waters.

Winslow knew Semmes well. They had served together on

the *Raritan* and fought together in the Mexican War. In other respects, they were opposites. Although a Southerner by birth, Winslow had been educated in New England and married a Boston woman. He also became an ardent abolitionist who believed in the moral duty of the North to eradicate slavery. The paunchy and balding Winslow was an excellent officer. With a well-trained crew he had spent a year searching for the

John A. Winslow: born North Carolina 1811; Winslow took his early education in New England, before securing a midshipman's position in the U.S. Navy through the offices of Daniel Webster in 1827; he saw a variety of duties in the Pacific, Atlantic, and Mediterranean, rising through the grades to commander by 1855; he lost the first ship under his command, the schooner *Morris*, in a storm off Tampico during the Mexican War; a man of religious piety and strong abolitionist beliefs, he was on shore duty at Boston at the outbreak of the Civil War; in December 1861 he was injured while commanding the riverboat *Benton* on the Mississippi and incapacitated for several months; he was embittered by the promotion over him of David Dixon Porter, and highly critical of the prosecution of the

war, believing the slavery issue more important than saving the Union; he was nonetheless promoted to captain in July 1862 and later that year took command of the *Kearsarge*; throughout 1863 and 1864 he patrolled the Atlantic; in June 1864 he caught the infamous Confederate raider *Alabama* in port at Cherbourg, France; Rebel Captain Raphael Semmes offered battle, and after a brief but ferocious fight the *Alabama* was sunk; although Semmes escaped, Winslow became a national hero; returning to the United States, he passed the balance of the war capitalizing on his celebrity to stimulate public support for the conflict; promoted to commodore to date from his victory over Semmes, he commanded the Gulf Squadron after the war; in 1870 he was elevated to rear admiral and given command of the Pacific Fleet; declining health forced Admiral Winslow's retirement from active duty in 1872, but he was carried on the active list until his death at Boston the following year.

The U.S.S. *Kearsarge*

Alabama and he was determined that she would not again elude him. He ordered a gun fired to recall his crew ashore and the *Kearsarge* was soon underway.

The *Kearsarge*, two months out of a Dutch dockyard and in excellent condition, arrived at Cherbourg on June 14 and quickly located the *Alabama*. Winslow sent a boat ashore to request French authorities to hand over the prisoners just released. Semmes objected on the grounds that this could augment the *Kearsarge*'s crew in a forthcoming battle, with which the French authorities concurred. Winslow then took the *Kearsarge* off the breakwater, where she took up station without anchoring in order to prevent the *Alabama* from escaping.

Despite the fact that his ship was in poor condition and slowed by her foul bottom Semmes did not hesitate to do battle. Immediately on sighting the *Kearsarge* he ordered 100 tons of coal delivered and set his crew to work preparing for an engagement. It was partly a matter of pride; the war was about up and there had been little glory in sinking merchantmen. In any case, Semmes had little choice. Delay would bring more Union warships. Indeed, Winslow had already telegraphed Lisbon to ask the commander of the heavily armed sailing sloop *St. Louis* (four VIII-inch, 55cwt shell guns, twelve 32-pounders of 33cwt, two 20-pounder rifles, and one 12-pounder smoothbore) to join him at Cherbourg.

Semmes sent a sarcastic message to Confederate agent M. Bonfils at Cherbourg: "I desire you to say to the U.S. consul that my intention is to fight the *Kearsarge* as soon as I can make the necessary arrangements. I hope these will not detain me more than tomorrow evening or after the morrow morning at the furthest. I beg she will not depart before I am ready to go out."

Semmes also communicated with his superior, Commodore Samuel Barron, the senior Confederate Navy officer in Europe, who was then in Paris, and received permission to use his own discretion. Meanwhile, he and his crew did all they could to prepare the *Alabama*. Semmes took on a full load of coal—filled bunkers would help protect the machinery from shot. Nonessential spars and rigging were removed, the deck holystoned (scoured), small arms and swords cleaned, and the crew put through gunnery drill. Semmes took the precaution of sending ashore the ship's valuables: his collection of chronometers taken out of each of his captures, all the *Alabama's* gold (about 4,700 gold sovereigns), her payroll, and the ten ransom bonds on ships he had released. As a point of pride, however, he kept aboard the ship his collection of flags from his prizes.

Semmes informed French authorities that he would be fighting the next day and then he attended Mass. As a precautionary measure he advised his men to make their wills. That night there were farewell parties for the *Alabama's* crew in Cherbourg cafés, although the men apparently behaved well and turned in early. The next morning they were not allowed to do any work until nine o'clock when the boilers were lit and Semmes called the crew aft and addressed them for the last time:

> Officers and Seamen of the *Alabama*: You have at length another opportunity of meeting the enemy—the first that has been presented to you since you sank the *Hatteras*. In the meantime, you have been all over the world, and it is not too much to say that you have destroyed, and driven for protection under neutral flags, one half of the enemy's commerce, which, at the beginning of the war, covered every sea. This is an achievement of which you may well be proud; and a grateful country will not be unmindful of it. The name of your ship has become a household word wherever civilization extends. Shall that name be tarnished by defeat? The thing is impossible! Remember that you are on the English Channel, the

theatre of so much of the naval glory of our race, and that the eyes of all Europe are at this moment upon you. The flag that floats over you is that of a young Republic, who bids defiance to her enemies, whenever, and wherever found. Show the world that you know how to uphold it! Go to your quarters.

The ship was then made ready for battle and gun crews stripped to the waist. Semmes wore his dress uniform. Throughout the battle he was on the quarterdeck, just before the mizzenmast. As the *Alabama* steamed out of the harbor it passed the French ship of the line *Napoléon*, the band of which struck up "Dixie" while her sailors cheered.

Sunday June 19, 1864, was a perfect day, partly hazy, with a calm sea and light wind from the west. The French sent their ironclad *Couronne* to escort the *Alabama* and assure there would be no violations of French territorial waters in the ensu-

John Lancaster

ing fight. The two ships left Cherbourg harbor about 9:30 A.M. In their wake were several other craft, the most prominent of which was the *Deerhound*, a yacht owned by John Lancaster, a pro-Southern Englishman. Lancaster's family had been in France and he had ordered her captain, Evan P. Jones, to pick them up at Cherbourg. Faced with the impending events, the family met to decide whether they should stay in port or go out to witness the battle. Lancaster's nine-year-old daughter was said to have cast the deciding vote.

The battle between the U.S.S. *Kearsarge* and the C.S.S. *Alabama* in the English Channel off Cherbourg was

Spectators viewing action off the coast of Cherbourg, France

one the most spectacular of Civil War naval engagements. It was also unusual in that an estimated 15,000 people observed it from the cliffs and the windows of houses ashore, although most saw the battle only as smoky smudges on the horizon.

There are numerous etchings and paintings of the battle, including one by impressionist master Edouard Manet. At the beginning of his career, Manet had traveled from Paris to Cherbourg and may have gotten a place on one of the French pilot boats, from which he drew the sketches that he used in his painting.

Despite Semmes's later claims that the *Kearsarge* had the advantage in size, weight of ordnance, and number of guns and crew, the two ships were actually closely matched. Semmes admitted as much in a journal entry of June 15: "My crew seems to be in the right spirit, a quiet spirit of determination, pervading both officers and men. The combat will no doubt be contested and obstinate, but the two ships are so equally matched that I do not feel at liberty to decline it. God defend the right and have mercy upon the souls of those who fall as many of us must."

Commissioned in January 1862, the *Kearsarge* weighed 1,550 tons. Her eleven knots maximum speed made her slightly faster than her opponent, and her crew complement was 160 men. For armament she carried in broadside four 32-pounder (42cwt) guns. She also mounted one 30-pounder rifled gun. A small 12-pounder, not included in her official armament, was also aboard. Her real strength, however, was in two XI-inch pivot-mounted smoothbore Dahlgren guns. Each threw 135-pound shell. The *Kearsarge* also had a more effective pivot mount. Traverse was facilitated in that the central bolt in the pivot mount was removed after the gun was rotated and then reinserted through the forward cross members into a designated metal collar on the deck on the side to which the gun was to be fired.

The *Kearsarge's* strength was in medium- to short-range

fire, while the *Alabama*, with her large Blakeley rifled gun, would have the advantage at long range. The *Kearsarge* mounted seven guns, but could fight only five on one side—the same number as the *Alabama*. The *Kearsarge*'s broadside weight of metal was about a quarter greater than that of her opponent (364 pounds to 274).

At about 10:20 A.M. a lookout on the *Kearsarge* spotted the *Alabama* coming out. Winslow had just begun reading Sunday service to the crew. When the officer of the deck shouted, "The *Alabama*!" he closed the prayer book, picked up a speaking trumpet, and ordered the crew beat to quarters. Winslow had the *Kearsarge* steam off to the northeast. He did this not only to ensure that the battle would occur sufficiently outside French territorial waters but so that his ship would be able to prevent the *Alabama* from running back to the French shore should she try to do so. Semmes and the *Alabama* followed. Both ships had hammocks stowed along their rails to provide some protection against small arms fire. Meanwhile, the *Couronne* took up position at the three-mile French territorial limit.

Semmes expected to use his starboard guns in broadside and shifted one 32-pounder from the port side to strengthen that battery. The added weight caused the *Alabama* to list about two feet on her starboard side, but this was thought to be an advantage as it exposed less of that side of the vessel to enemy fire.

When the two ships were about a mile and a quarter apart Winslow reversed course and headed for the *Alabama*. He, too, planned to use his starboard battery, so the two ships met one another going in opposite directions.

The battle began some six or seven miles offshore, well beyond the three-mile French territorial limit. The entire action lasted a little longer than an hour. At 10:57 Semmes opened with a broadside at somewhat less than a mile. It was several minutes, two or three Confederate broadsides (all of which passed high), and the range was down to about a half-mile, before the *Kearsarge* replied. Both commanders subsequently claimed they had wanted to close while their antagonist had sought to avoid it. Winslow ordered a port turn to try to place his own ship in position to rake the *Alabama*. Semmes veered his ship to port to avoid this but his maneuver allowed Winslow to close the range. As the *Alabama* turned back to starboard the *Kearsarge* mirrored her movement. The *Kearsarge* was faster and Winslow sought to narrow the range; thus the circles grew progressively smaller from one-half to one-quarter of a mile in diameter with each ship firing her starboard batteries only. As they circled the ships gradually drifted westward in the current.

The *Alabama* had the early advantage as her large Blakeley rifle had longer range than any of her opponent's guns. The Federals were very lucky in that one Blakeley shell failed to explode. It lodged in the *Kearsarge*'s wooden sternpost and had it gone off it would have destroyed her steering and made her unmanageable (later the section of the sternpost with the unexploded shell still embedded was given to the Naval Academy Museum; it is now in the Washington Navy Yard Museum). Semmes wrote that if the fuse had worked, "I should have been called upon to save Captain Winslow's crew from drowning." Even so the *Kearsarge*'s steering became so difficult that it took four men to move the rudder.

One advantage for the *Kearsarge* came from 120 fathoms of chain strung over the vital middle parts of his ship to protect her engines, boilers, and magazines from enemy fire; this technique had been proven in fighting along the Mississippi River and the chain had been in place on the *Kearsarge* for some time. An outward sheathing of one-inch wood painted the same color as the rest of the hull concealed this from Confederate observation, but the French had informed Semmes about it. In effect, the *Kearsarge* was a partial ironclad.

The *Alabama* had chain in her lockers that might have been used for the same purpose. Later Semmes claimed he had been unaware of the *Kearsarge's* chain mail, which he said was an unfair advantage in that it made her a "concealed ironclad." He seems to have convinced himself that this was the only reason the *Alabama* lost the battle. But as historian George W. Dalzell noted, "This is a curious misconception of the character of warfare to take possession of the mind of a professional naval officer of life-long training, whose own vessel was born in deception and who for nearly two years had been disguising her with false colors to decoy unarmed merchantmen."

Lieutenant Sinclair wrote that Semmes knew about the chain and he was critical of him for not equipping the *Alabama* in the same fashion:

> Winslow, for protecting his ship with chain-armor, should, in the humble judgment of the writer, submitted with diffidence, be accounted as simply using proper prudence in the direct line of duty. He had not given, accepted, or declined a challenge. But it was his duty to fight if he could, and win. Semmes knew all about it, and could have adopted the same scheme. It was not his election to do so.

Semmes followed the action by means of a spyglass and could see that the *Alabama's* shot that did strike were having no effect on the chain-protected side of the *Kearsarge* (these tore holes in the wood covering but did not pierce the heavy chain beneath). He ordered the gun crews to fire higher. One shell tore through the *Kearsarge's* smokestack; another sheared off the top of the engine-room hatch. Only one shot from the Confederate vessel caused personnel casualties aboard the *Kearsarge*: a Blakeley shell that exploded on the quarterdeck wounded three men at the after pivot gun, one mortally.

As the range narrowed, both sides substituted shell for solid shot. Semmes hoped to close the range on his opponent sufficiently to take the *Kearsarge* by boarding. Winslow refused to oblige and instead kept to a range that would allow his own guns to be most effective. Throughout the battle Winslow was able to dictate its range because his vessel was both faster and more maneuverable than his opponent's.

Shell from the two XI-inch Dahlgren guns now began to tear into the *Alabama* and have a terrible effect on the ship and her crew. The raider's hull was repeatedly hit and shell ripped large holes in her side. Lieutenant Sinclair of the *Alabama* noted, "The boarding tactics of Semmes having been frustrated, and we unable to pierce the enemy's hull with our fire, nothing can place victory with us but some unforeseen and lucky turn." The fire from the *Kearsarge* wreaked havoc on the *Alabama*:

> ...our bulwarks are soon shot away in sections; and the after pivot-gun is disabled on its port side, losing, in killed and wounded, all but the compresser-man. The quarter-deck thirty-two pounder of this division is now secured, and the crew sent to man the pivot-gun. The spar-deck is by this time being rapidly torn up by shell bursting on the between-decks, interfering with working our battery; and the compartments below have all been knocked into one. The *Alabama* is making water fast, showing severe punishment....An 11-inch shell enters us at the water-line, in the wake of the writer's gun, and passes on, explodes in the engine- room, in its passage throwing a volume of water on board, hiding for a moment the guns of this division. Our ship trembles from stem to stern from the blow. Semmes at once sends for the engineer on watch, who reports the fires out, and water beyond the control of the pumps.

During the seventh circle Semmes was slightly wounded in the right hand by a shell fragment. A quartermaster bandaged the wound and rigged a sling for him.

At the beginning of the eighth circle, when the two ships were about four hundred yards apart, Semmes saw that his ship was in sinking condition and turned her out of the circle, ordering Lieutenant Kell to set all sail in hopes of making the French shore. He also opened fire with his port battery, but the *Alabama* was taking on too much water. Semmes was able to bring only two port guns to bear and the *Alabama* was now completely at the mercy of the *Kearsarge*, the accuracy of her fire having increased as the battle wore on. Winslow, having closed the range, was preparing to fire grape shot.

Sinclair described the *Alabama*'s last minutes: "The ship is settling in her spar-deck, and her wounded spars are stagger-

Combat between the *Alabama* and the *Kearsarge*

ing in the "steps," held only by the rigging. Her decks present a woful appearance, torn up in innumerable holes, and air-bubbles rising and bursting, producing a sound as though the boat was in agony."

Lieutenant Kell, sent below to check on conditions there, reported to Semmes that the *Alabama* could not last ten minutes. Semmes ordered him to cease firing, shorten sail, and haul down the colors. Semmes then sent a dinghy to the *Kearsarge* to notify Winslow that he was ready to surrender. Semmes and Sinclair later wrote that the *Kearsarge* continued to fire on his ship after her colors were struck and a white flag displayed; Winslow asserted that he had ordered fire halted when the *Alabama*'s colors came down and a white flag was raised at her stern, but that shortly afterward the Confederate ship had opened fire again, from the two guns on the port side. Winslow said he then moved his ship into position to rake his antagonist but, seeing the white flag still flying, he had again held fire.

With his vessel in a sinking condition Semmes ordered "All hands save yourselves" to be piped. All but two of the *Alabama*'s boats had been destroyed in the battle and one of these two had been damaged. Most men simply leaped in the sea. Semmes gave his papers to a sailor who was a good swimmer, and then jumped in himself.

The *Alabama* sank in about fifteen minutes, stern first, at 12:24 P.M., according to the *Kearsarge*'s log. Surgeon John M. Browne of the *Kearsarge* described her last moments:

> She was severely hulled between her main and mizzen masts and settled by the stern; the main mast, pierced by a shot at the very last, broke off near the head and went over the side, the bow lifted high from the water; then came the end. Suddenly assuming a perpendicular position caused by the falling aft of the battery and the stores, she went down, the jib boom

being the last to appear above water....As she disap-
peared to her last resting place, there was no cheer
[on the *Kearsarge*]; all was silent.

Broadside fire from each ship had been largely ineffective
in the outcome. Perhaps surprisingly, the *Alabama* got off
many more shots, 370, but only some 30 of them struck their
opponent (13 in and about the hull and 16 in the masts and
rigging). They did little damage and caused no casualties other
than the three men at the pivot gun. This low total is indeed
surprising, given that six of the *Alabama*'s gunners had been
trained on the Royal Navy gunnery ship
Excellent.

Having incurred little damage, the
Kearsarge was perfectly ready to fight
again. Winslow reported that during
the battle she had fired 173 shots, of
which a high percentage struck.
Semmes later said that one shot alone
killed or wounded eighteen men at the
after pivot gun. The superior Union
gunnery was probably attributable to
excellent training by executive officer
Lieutenant Commander James S.
Thornton. After the battle Winslow said
it would have been over more quickly
had he been able to close earlier.

Shell fire from the heavy XI-inch
pivot guns of the Union vessel had
decided the engagement, especially a
fortunate shot that damaged the
Alabama's steering apparatus. The
Alabama's crew did labor under the
disadvantage of weakened powder. In
all there were forty-one casualties

James S. Thornton: became
a midshipman in the U.S.
Navy in 1841; passed mid-
shipman in 1847; promoted
to acting master in 1855;
promoted to lieutenant on
the active list in 1855; promoted successively to lieutenant commander in 1862;
to commander in 1866; and
to captain in 1872; he died
in 1875.

aboard the Confederate vessel: nine men dead and twenty wounded in action, and twelve men drowned.

Winslow was slow to order his ship to pick up survivors. Part of the reason for this was that most of his own boats had been badly damaged in the battle by the high Confederate fire. Finally the launch and second cutter were gotten down. The result of the delay and lack of boats, however, was that many of the men in the water were taken aboard neutral ships. Some were hauled aboard French pilot boats.

The *Deerhound*, which had been about a mile away during the battle, ran under the stern of the *Kearsarge* and Lancaster volunteered to pick up survivors, to which Winslow agreed. She rescued forty-two men, including Semmes and executive officer Kell, all of whom she took to Southampton. London rejected Minister Adams's demands that Semmes and his crew be turned over to U.S. authorities. British Foreign Minister Lord John Russell replied,

> It appears to me that the owner of the *Deerhound* performed only a common duty of humanity in saving from the waves the captain and several of the crew of the *Alabama*. They would otherwise, in all probability, have been drowned, and thus would never have been in the situation of prisoners of war. It does not appear to me to be any part of the duty of a neutral

The *Deerhound* rescuing survivors of the *Alabama*

to assist in making prisoners of war for one of the belligerents.

Lancaster, the *Deerhound*'s owner, pointed out that Winslow had asked him to rescue the *Alabama*'s crew, shouting to him: "For God's sake do what you can to save them!" Porter claimed that the *Deerhound* had departed the scene with many men still in the water because Semmes, fearful that Winslow would demand that he be turned over, pleaded with Lancaster to save him. But Porter also criticized Secretary of the Navy Welles for placing too much importance on Semmes's escape "than the matter deserved" and blaming Captain Winslow "for his course in paroling the prisoners," whom he classified as "pirates." Unfairly, Semmes blamed Winslow for his men who drowned: "Ten of my men were permitted to drown."

The wounded men from the *Alabama* were saved because they were put in the *Alabama*'s boats and sent to the *Kearsarge*. Assistant Surgeon David Llewellyn could have gone with them but refused and was drowned. He could not swim and so the crew rigged a makeshift life preserver for him of shell boxes. These were tied to his waist but apparently raised the middle of his body higher in the water than his head, so that he drowned before a boat reached him. Among those also drowned was David White, Llewellyn's African American servant; he, too, could not swim. Lieutenant Arthur Sinclair was among those hauled into the *Kearsarge*'s boats. He later said that on realizing the situation they were in he and one of the *Alabama*'s seamen slipped quietly over the side and swam to a boat belonging to the *Deerhound*. In all the *Kearsarge* took aboard from the *Alabama* six officers and sixty-four men (including twenty wounded). Winslow took them all to Cherbourg where he paroled them.

Raphael Semmes after the loss of the *Alabama*

9
AFTER THE BATTLE

Semmes and the *Alabama* survivors who landed in Britain were lionized and feted there. Among other honors, British officers presented Semmes with a handsome new sword. Undoubtedly some of the adulation had to do with the fact that the *Alabama* was British built and most of her crew were British. Semmes paid off his remaining crew and sent allotments to the relatives of the dead. After some weeks Semmes went to the Continent; he visited Belgium, including the battlefield at Waterloo, and Switzerland to rest. At the end of September he returned to London and on October 3 embarked on the steamer *Tasmanian* for Havana via St. Thomas. He changed ships at St. Thomas and went on to Havana, where he arrived at the end of October and took passage on a small former U.S. ship recently transferred to British registry, landing at the town of Bagdad at the mouth of the Rio Grande on the Mexican side of the Texas border.

Semmes returned to the Confederacy by way of Brownsville and then made his way to Richmond. Promoted to rear admiral in February 1865, Semmes received command of the James River Squadron of three ironclad rams and seven wooden steamers. His final naval command lasted barely three months. The squadron's anchorage was largely immune from attack as long as it was protected by powerful shore batteries, but when Confederate forces abandoned Richmond, Semmes had no choice but to destroy his ships. Accordingly, on the night of April 2, 1865, they were set on fire, scuttled, or blown up. The men of the squadron then formed into a naval brigade under Semmes as a brigadier general. The brigade retreated to Greensboro, North Carolina, where it joined General Joseph E. Johnston's army and later surrendered.

Paroled on May 1, 1865, Semmes returned to Mobile, where on December 15 he was arrested by order of Secretary Welles, despite the protection his parole should have afforded. He was transported to Washington and held there for three months. Apparently the plan was to try him before a military commission on charges that he had violated military codes by escaping from the *Alabama* after her colors had been struck. After the Supreme Court denied jurisdiction of such commissions, charges against Semmes were dropped and he again returned home. He was briefly probate judge of Mobile County, but was forced out of that office. Semmes then accepted the chair of moral philosophy and English Literature at Louisiana State Seminary (now Louisiana State University) at Baton Rouge. Political pressure again forced him out. He then became editor of the *Memphis Daily Bulletin* until he was hounded from that post as well. After a profitable lecture tour he resumed the practice of law. In 1869 he published *Memoirs of Service Afloat, During the War between the States.* Semmes died on August 30, 1877, and is buried in Mobile.

In the United States, Captain Winslow was lionized. On Lincoln's recommendation Congress extended a vote of thanks and approved his promotion to commodore, dating from the day of his victory, June 19. Secretary of the Navy Welles was none too happy with him and rather unfairly blamed Winslow for Semmes's escape and for paroling the prisoners, which implied recognition of belligerent status for the Confederate raider. Winslow, who pointed out to Welles that he had no room aboard his ship for prisoners, later retired from the navy a rear admiral. Lieutenant Commander Thornton, on the other hand, was slighted. He was advanced only ten numbers in grade, although Winslow had singled him out for praise and it was well known that it was largely his work in training the gun crews that caused the engagement to be so short.

The defeat of the *Alabama* signalled the beginning of the end for Confederate commerce raiders. The *Florida*, commissioned before the *Alabama*, was active in the Atlantic. Her career ended on the night of October 7, 1864, when she was in Bahia harbor, Brazil. She was rammed and captured there in defiance of Brazilian neutrality by the U.S. Navy screw sloop *Wachusett* (Captain Napoleon Collins). The C.S.S. *Shenandoah*, another Bulloch purchase, was active in the Pacific and Arctic Oceans. Most of her captures came after the conclusion of hostilities. James T. Waddell, her captain, refused to believe early newspaper accounts that the war was over. Finally convinced of the fact in August 1865, he then sailed his ship 17,000 miles to London and there surrendered to British authorities. The *Shenandoah* enjoyed the distinction of being the only Confederate ship to circumnavigate the globe.

As early as November 1862 U.S. Minister Adams in London had filed claims with the British Government for losses suffered by Northern shipping, and after the Civil War the issue of the British government having allowed the fitting out of the *Alabama* and other Confederate cruisers became a major stumbling block in Anglo-American relations. British officials and capital had backed the wrong side. Washington believed, rightly or wrongly, that London's speedy proclamation of neutrality and then persistent disregard of it in the early period of the war had heartened the South and prolonged the conflict.

The powerful chairman of the Senate Committee on Foreign Relations, Charles Sumner, asserted that Britain owed the United States half the cost of the war, or some $2.5 billion. He proposed the solution of taking British Western Hemisphere possessions, including Canada, as compensation.

Little was done to meet U.S. demands for compensation until 1871, the year the German states defeated France. The European balance of power was decisively changed and in January of that year Prussian Minister President Otto von Bismarck proclaimed at Versailles the establishment of the German Empire. Britain found itself increasingly isolated. Statesmen in London believed it might be wise to reach some accommodation with the United States against the possibility of a German drive for world, as opposed to European, hegemony. London then proposed an arbitration tribunal. The Treaty of Washington, dated May 8, 1871, expressed "in a friendly spirit the regret felt by Her Majesty's Government for the escape under whatever circumstances of the *Alabama* and other vessels from British ports and the depredations committed by these vessels."

A tribunal was then set up. Consisting of five representatives (one each from Britain, the United States, Brazil, Switzerland, and Italy), it met in Geneva beginning on December 15, 1871, to hear and determine "claims growing out of the acts committed" by the *Alabama* and the other Confederate commerce raiders fitted out in Britain "and generally known as the *Alabama* claims." The commission did throw out Washington's claims arising out of indirect damages such as U.S. expenditures in pursuit of the cruisers, the transfer of U.S. shipping to British registry, and any prolongation of the war. Nevertheless, on September 14, 1872, the tribunal awarded the United States Government $15,500,500 in damages. A special U.S. court was then set up to disperse the funds and ultimately awarded $9,416,120.25. This left a considerable amount unawarded; augmented by interest on bonds in which the fund was invested, it soon came to more than $10 million. Talk of returning this to Britain was quashed in favor of setting up another claims court authorized to make payments beyond those cases covered by the Geneva tribunal. Anything remaining was to be used to refund premiums paid by shippers for war insurance. Direct losses were indeed paid in full and insurance charges prorated. The *Alabama* claims settlement has been regarded as an important step forward in the peaceful settlement of international disputes and a victory for the rule of law.

During the Civil War the *Alabama* and other Confederate commerce raiders destroyed some 257 Union merchant ships, or about 5 percent of the total. They succeeded in driving up insurance rates substantially but hardly disrupted U.S. trade, and they did not disturb the Union blockade, which became steadily more effective as the war progressed.

The main effect of the commerce raiders was to force a substantial number of vessels into permanent foreign registry. In 1860 two-thirds of the trade of the port of New York was in U.S.-registry vessels; three years later the percentage had fallen to only one-fourth. During four years of war more than seven hundred U.S. ships transferred to British registry alone.

George Dalzell concluded that the *Alabama* and her sisters had inflicted "irreparable injury" to the U.S. merchant marine in causing the flight of so many U.S. vessels to foreign registry. He concluded that more than half of the total U.S. merchant fleet was permanently lost to the flag during the Civil War. The cruisers burned or sank 110,000 tons but another 800,000 tons was sold to foreign owners—and these were the best ships. The ones left were those the foreigners did not want.

Two final notes. The *Kearsarge* was wrecked off Roncador Reef, Central America, on February 2, 1894. Her name lives on in the U.S. Navy, however, in the amphibious assault ship

Kearsarge. And on November 7, 1984, the French minesweeper *Circé* located the wreckage of the *Alabama* off Cherbourg at a depth of slightly less than 200 feet about six miles off the coast in what are now French territorial waters. Since 1978 the French Navy had been looking specifically for the *Alabama* wreck as a test for sonar operators.

Although she is within French territorial waters, British preservationist groups want the wreck, if it is raised, to be displayed at Birkenhead where the *Alabama* was built and where the British Government has ordered Number 4 Dockyard preserved as a historical site specifically for that purpose. The United States Government also asserts ownership of the wreck, and in 1989 Congress passed the C.S.S. *Alabama* Preservation Act. The fight over the *Alabama* continues.

APPENDIX

PRIZES TAKEN BY THE *SUMTER* AND THE *ALABAMA*

Note: The lists of prizes presented in the appendix are taken from *Official Records of the Union and Confederate Navies in the War of the Rebelliom*, Series I, Volumes 1 and 3; and Paul H. Silverstone, *Warships of the Civil War Navies* (Annapolis, MD.: Naval Institute Press, 1989).

All ships listed were sailing vessels, unless otherwise noted. Ships marked with an asertisk were destroyed.

SUMTER PRIZES

1. *Golden Rocket** (July 3, 1861)
2. *Cuba* (July 4, 1861)
3. *Machias* (July 4, 1861)
4. *Albert Adams* (July 5,1861)
5. *Ben Dunning* (July 5, 1861)
6. *Lewis Kilham* (July 25, 1861)
7. *Naiad* (July 25, 1861)
8. *West Wind* (July 25, 1861)
9. *Abbie Bradford* (July 25, 1861)
10. *Joseph Maxwell* (July 27, 1861)
11. *Joseph Park** (September 25, 1861)
12. *Daniel Trowbridge** (October 27, 1861)
13. *Montmorency* (November 25, 1861: bond of $20,000)
14. *Arcade** (November 26, 1861)
15. *Vigilent** (December 3, 1861)
16. *Ebenezer Dodge** (December 8, 1861)
17. *Investigator* (January 18, 1862)
18. *Neapolitan** (January 28, 1862)

ALABAMA PRIZES
(VALUE IS THAT OF CONDEMNATION PROCEEDINGS)

1. *Ocmulgee** (September 5, 1862: $50,000)
2. *Starlight** (September 7, 1962: $4,000)
3. *Ocean Rover** (September 8, 1862: $70,000)
4. *Alert** (September 9, 1862: $20,000)
5. *Weather Gauge** (September 9, 1862: $10,000)
6. *Altamaha** (September 13, 1862: $3,000)
7. *Benjamin Tucker** (September 14, 1862: $18,000)
8. *Courser** (September 16, 1862: $7,000)
9. *Virginia** (September 17, 1862: $25,000)
10. *Elisha Dunbar** (September 18, 1862: $25,000)
11. *Brilliant** (October 3, 1862: $164,000)
12. *Emily Farnham* (October 3, 1862: cartel, no bond)
13. *Wave Crest** (October 7, 1862: $44,000)
14. *Dunkirk** (October 7, 1862: $25,000)
15. *Tonawanda* (October 9, 1862: bond of $80,000)
16. *Manchester** (October 11, 1862: $164,000)
17. *Lamplighter** (October 15, 1862: $117,600)
18. *Lafayette** (October 23, 1862: vessel, $49,000; cargo, $51,337)
19. *Crenshaw** (October 26, 1862: vessel, $11,680; cargo, $22,189)
20. *Lauraetta** (October 28, 1862: vessel, $15,000; cargo, $17,880)
21. *Baron de Custine* (October 29, 1862: bond of $6,000)
22. *Levi Starbuck** (November 2, 1862: $25,000)
23. *Thomas B. Wales** (November 8, 1862: $246,625)
24. *Clara L. Sparks** (November 21, 1862)
25. *Parker Cook** (November 30, 1862: $10,000)

26. *Nina* (December 5, 1862)

27. *Union* (December 5, 1862: bond of $1,500)

28. Steamer *Ariel* (December 7, 1862: bond of $261,000)

29. *Golden Rule** (January 26, 1863: $112,000)

30. *Chastelaine** (January 27, 1863: $10,000)

31 *Palmetto** (February 3, 1863: $18,430)

32. *Golden Eagle** (February 21, 1863: $61,000)

33. *Olive Jane** (February 21, 1863: $43,208)

34. *Washington** (February 27, 1863: bond of $50,000)

35. *Bethia Thayer** (March 1, 1863: bond of $40,000)

36. *John A. Parke** (March 2, 1863: $66,157)

37. *Punjab* (March 15, 1863: bond of $55,000)

38. *Morning Star* (March 23, 1863: bond of $61,750)

39. *Kingfisher** (March 23, 1863: $2,400)

40. *Charles Hill* (March 25, 1863: $28,450)

41. *Nora** (March 25, 1863: $76,636)

42. *Louisa Hatch** (April 4, 1863: $38,315)

43. *Kate Cory** (April 15, 1863: $10,568)

44. *Lafayette** (April 15, 1863: $20,908)

45. *Nye** (April 24, 1863: $31,127)

46. Steamer *Dorcas Prince** (April 26, 1863: $44,108)

47. *Sea Lark** (May 3, 1863: $550,000)

48. *Union Jack** (May 3, 1863: $77,000)

49. *Justina* (May 25, 1863: bond of $7,000)

50. *Gildersleeve** (May 25, 1863: vessel, $60,000; cargo, $2,783)

51. *Jabez Snow** (May 29, 1863: vessel, $68,672; cargo, $4,109)

52. *Amazonian** (June 2, 1863: $97,665)

53. *Talisman** (June 5, 1863: $139,195)

54. *Conrad* (June 20, 1863: vessel, $15,000; cargo, $85,936)

55. *Anna F. Schmidt** (July 2, 1863: $350,000)

56. *Express** (July 6, 1863: vessel, $57,000; cargo: $64,300)

57. *Sea Bride* (August 5, 1863: sold for $16,940)

58. *Amanda** (November 6, 1863: vessel, $41,860; cargo, $62,582)

59. *Winged Racer** (November 10, 1863: vessel, $87,000; cargo, $63,000)

60. *Contest** (November 11, 1863: $72,815; cargo, $50,000)

61. *Martaban* (ex *Texas Star*)* (December 24, 1863: $97,628)

62. *Highlander** (December 26, 1863: $75,965)

63. *Sonora** (December 26, 1863: $46,545)

64. *Emma Jane** (January 14, 1864: $40,000)

65. *Rockingham** (April 23, 1864: $97,878)

66. *Tycoon** (April 27, 1864: $390,000)

TUSCALOOSA PRIZES

(ex-*Conrad*, tender to the *Alabama*)

1. *Santee* (July 31, 1963)

2. *Living Age* (September 13, 1863)

FURTHER READING

DOCUMENTS

Alabama File. W.S. Hoole Special Collections Library,
    University of Alabama, Tuscaloosa.
*Official Records of the Union and Confederate Navies in the War
of the Rebellion.* Series I, Volumes 1–3: *The Operations of the
    Cruisers.* Washington, D.C.: Government Printing Office,
    1894–96.

BOOKS

Adams, Charles Francis. *A Cycle of Adams Letters,
    1861–1865.* Edited by Worthington C. Ford. 2 vols. Boston:
    Houghton Mifflin, 1920.
_____. *Charles Francis Adams.* Boston: Houghton Mifflin, 1900.
Appleton's Cyclopaedia of American Biography. Edited by Grant
    Wilson and John Fiske. Vol. 4, pp. 458–60. New York: D.
    Appleton and Company, 1888.
Bennett, Frank M. *The Monitor and the Navy Under Steam.*
    New York: Houghton Mifflin, 1900.
Bennett, William E. *Cruise of a Corsair.* London: Cassell, 1963.
Boykin, Edward. *Ghost Ship of the Confederacy: The Story of
    the Alabama and Her Captain, Raphael Semmes.* New York:
    Funk & Wagnalls, 1957.
Bulloch, James Dunwody. *The Secret Service of the Confederate
    States in Europe.* 2 vols. New York: G.P. Putnam, 1884.
Captain Raphael Semmes and the C.S.S. Alabama. Washington:
    The Naval Historical Foundation, 1968.
Cockerham, Lynnwood M. *Raphael Semmes: A Leadership
    Study.* Maxwell AFB, AL: Air Command and Staff College,
    Air University, 1986.
Cook, Adrian. *The Alabama Claims: American Politics and
    Anglo-American Relations, 1865–1872.* Ithaca, N.Y.:
    Cornell University Press, 1975.

Dalzell, George W. *The Flight from the Flag: The Continuing Effect of the Civil War upon the American Carrying Trade.* Chapel Hill, NC: University of North Carolina Press, 1940.

Davis, Evangeline and Burke Davis. *Rebel Raider. A Biography of Admiral Semmes.* New York: J.B. Lippincott, 1973.

Delaney, Norman C. *Ghost Ship: the Confederate Raider Alabama.* Middletown, CN: Southfarm Press, 1989.

_____. *John McIntosh Kell of the Raider Alabama.* University, AL: University of Alabama Press, 1973.

Dictionary of American Biography. Edited by Dumas Malone. Vol. 16, pp. 590–82. New York: Charles Scribner's Sons, 1935.

Dictionary of American Military Biography. Vol. 3, pp. 975–78. Edited by Roger S. Spiller. Westport, Conn: Greenwood Press, 1984.

Ellicott, John M. *The life of John Ancrum Winslow, Rear-Admiral, United States Navy, Who Commanded the U.S. Steamer "Kearsarge" in Her Action with the Confederate Cruiser "Alabama."* 2d ed. New York: G.P. Putnam's Sons, 1905.

Kell, John McIntosh. *Recollections of a Naval Life.* Washington: Neale Co., 1900.

Low, John. *The Logs of the C.S.S. Alabama and C.S.S. Tuscaloosa, 1862–1863.* University, AL: Confederate Publishing Company, 1972.

Meriwether, Colyer. *Raphael Semmes.* Philadelphia: G.W. Jacobs & Co., 1913.

Merli, Frank J. *Great Britain and the Confederate Navy, 1861–1865.* Bloomington, IN: Indiana University Press, 1970.

Merli, Frank J., ed. *Special Commemorative Naval issue, C.S.S. Alabama, 1864–1989.* Vol. 4. *Journal of Confederate History.* Brentwood, Tenn.: Southern Heritage Press, 1989.

The National Cyclopaedia of American Biography. Vol. 4., pp. 340–41. New York: James T. White & Company, 1897.

Porter, Admiral David D. *Naval History of the Civil War.* Reprint ed., Secaucus, NJ: Castle Books, 1984.

Roberts, Walter A. *Semmes of the Alabama.* New York: The Bobbs-Merrill Company, 1938.

Robinson, Charles M., III. *Shark of the Confederacy. The Story of the C.S.S. Alabama.* Annapolis, MD: Naval Institute Press, 1995.

Robinson, William M., Jr. *The Confederate Privateers.* New Haven, Conn.: Yale University Press, 1928. Reprint ed., Columbia, SC: University of South Carolina Press, 1990.

Semmes, Raphael. *The Confederate Raider, Alabama; Selections from Memoirs of Service Afloat During the War Between the States.* Edited with an introduction by Philip Van Doren Stern. Greenwich, CN: Fawcett Publications, 1962.

_____. *The Cruise of the Alabama and the Sumter. From the Private Journals and Other Papers of Commander R. Semmes, C.S.N. and Other Officers.* 2 vols. London: Saunders, Otley & Company, 1864.

_____. *Memoirs of Service Afloat, During the War between the States.* Baltimore: Kelly, Piet & Co., 1869. Reprint ed., Secaucus, NJ: The Blue & Grey Press, 1987.

_____. *Raphael Semmes, Rear Admiral, Confederate States Navy, Brigadier General, Confederate States Army: Documents Pertaining to the Charges Preferred against Him by the United States Government: With a Pictorial History of the Voyages of the Sumter and Alabama and the Alabama Claims Commission.* Mobile, AL: Museum of the City of Mobile, 1978.

_____. *Service Afloat and Ashore During the Mexican War.* Cincinnati: W. H. Moore & Co., 1951.

Silverstone, Paul H. *Warships of the Civil War Navies.* Annapolis, MD: Naval Institute Press, 1989.

Sinclair, Arthur. *Two Years on the Alabama.* Boston: Lee and

Shepard, 1895.

Soley, James Russell. *The Blockade and the Cruisers*. New York: Charles Scribner's Sons, 1983.

Stern, Philip Van Doren. *The Confederate Navy. A Pictorial History*. Garden City, NY: Doubleday & Company, Inc., 1962.

Still, William N., Jr. *Confederate Shipbuilding*. Reprint ed., Columbia, SC: University of South Carolina Press, 1987.

Summersell, Charles G. *CSS Alabama: Builder, Captain, and Plans*. University, AL: University of Alabama Press, 1985.

_____. *The cruise of C.S.S. Sumter*. Tuscaloosa, Ala.: Confederate Publishing Co., 1965.

Taylor, John M. *Confederate Raider: Raphael Semmes of the Alabama*. Washington: Brassey's, 1994.

Tucker, Spencer C. *Arming the Fleet. U.S. Naval Ordnance in the Muzzle-loading Era*. Annapolis: U.S. Naval Institute Press, 1989.

U.S., Navy Department. *Civil War Naval Chronology, 1861–1865*. Washington: Naval History Division, 1971.

ARTICLES

Delaney, Norman C. "The End of the *Alabama*." *American Heritage* 23 (April 1972): 58–69, 102.

Merli, Frank J., ed. "Letters on the *Alabama*. June 1864," *Mariner's Mirror* 58 (May 1972): 216–18.

Robinson, William M., Jr. "The *Alabama-Kearsarge* Battle." *Essex Institute Historical Collections* 60 (April, July, 1924): 97–120, 209–18.

UNPUBLISHED MATERIALS

Eberly, Kurt J. "The Commerce Raider C.S.S. Alabama, 1862–1864." M.A. thesis, East Stroudsburg University, 1990.

PHOTO CREDITS

Sources and credits for photographs are as follows:

James D. Bulloch; James S. Thornton; John A.Winslow; Raphael Semmes. From *Battles and Leaders of the Civil War.* IV. (New York: Thomas Yoseloff, 1956).

John McIntosh Kell; John Lancaster; Arthur F. Sinclair; Lieutenants Armstrong and Sinclair on deck of the *Alabama.* From Arthur F. Sinclair, *Two Years on the Alabama.* (Boston: Lee and Shepard, 1895).

Raphael Semmes; Some of the officers who served on the Alabama; Combat between the *Alabama* and the *Hatteras.* From Raphael Semmes, *Memoirs of Service Afloat.* (Baltimore: Kelly, Piet, 1869).

C.S.S. *Alabama*; U.S.S. *Kearsarge*; C.S.S. *Sumter.* From *Official Record of the Union and Confederate Navies.* Series I, Volume I. (Government Printing Office, 1864).

Charles Francis Adams; The *Alabama* burns a prize. From *Harper's Weekly.*

Combat between the *Alabama* and the *Kearsarge*; Spectators viewing action off the coast of Cherbourg, France. From the United States Navy.

Chart tracking the battle between the *Alabama* and the *Kearsarge.* From David Porter, *The Naval History of the Civil War.* (New York: Sherman Publishing, 1886).

Gideon Welles. From Gideon Welles, *Diary of Gideon Welles.* Volume I. (Boston: Houghton Mifflin, 1911).

The *Deerhound* rescuing survivors of the *Alabama.* From the *Illustrated London News.*

Stephen R. Mallory. From the National Archives.

INDEX

Adams, Charles Francis, 33-35, 88, 93
Agrippina, 36-37, 39, 52-53, 60-61
Alabama (*Enrica*), 18, 19, 32-74, 76-78, 80-96
Alabama, prizes taken by, 99-101
Alabama Claims, 93-95
Anderson, L. R., 47
Ariel, 55
Armstrong, Richard, 47-48

Bahama, 36-37, 39
Bainbridge, 59
Baldwin, C. H., 61, 64
Banks, Nathaniel, 54, 56
Barron, Samuel, 76
Bell, Henry H., 56
Bismarck, Otto von, 94
Blake, Homer C., 56, 58
Bonfils, M., 76
Brooklyn, 27, 56
Browne, John M., 86
Bulloch, Irvine S., 47-48
Bulloch, James Dunwoody, 17, 20, 31-36, 39, 48
Butcher, Mathew J., 36

Chickamauga, 33
Circé, 96
Clarence 18
Collier, Robert P. 35
Collins, Napoleon 93
Conrad (see also *Tuscaloosa*), 18, 61
Contest, 66
Couronne, 78, 81
Craven, T. A., 35

Dalzell, George W. (quoted), 83, 95
Davis, Jefferson, 15, 22
Deerhound, 78, 88-89
Diomede, 62

Dudley, Thomas H., 33
Dunkirk, 49, 50

Edwards, Price, 36
Elisha Dunbar, 48
Excellent, 87

Fingal, 32-33, 35
Florida, 18, 31, 33, 35, 48, 60, 93
Freeman, Miles J., 48
Fullam, G. T., 47

Galt, Francis L., 48, 50
Georgia, 33, 60, 73
Golden Rocket, 28
Golden Rule, 59
Guerre de course, definition of, 15

Harding, John, 35
Hatteras, 56-58, 60, 77
Hercules, 36
Hope, James, 67
Howell, Beckett K., 47-48
Hull, F. S., 35

Kearsarge, 19, 60, 70-71, 72-78, 80-89, 95-96
Kell, John M., 46, 48, 85-86, 88

Iroquois, 29

Johnston, Joseph E., 92
Jones, Evan P,. 78

Laird, John, 31, 41
Lancaster, John, 78, 88-89
Lincoln, Abraham, 15, 65
Llewellyn, David, 89
Louisa Hatch, 60
Low, John, 61, 63

Mackenzie, A. S., 21
McDougal, David M., 67
Maffit, Eugene, 47, 48
Maffit, John N., 18, 33, 48
Mallory, Stephen R., 14, 15, 16, 17
Manchester, 49
Manet, Edouard, 80
Martaban (Texas Star), 67
Mason, James M., 29
Maury, Matthew Fontaine, 16
Mohican, 60-61
Mutiny, on board *Somers,* 21; on *Alabama,* 53
Myers, Henry, 44

Napoléon, 78
Napoleon III, 73

Ocmulgee, 42, 44

Poor, Charles, 27
Porter, David, 20, 27, 45, 52, 59, 62, 89
Powhatan, 27
Privateering, 15, 16

Rappahannock, 73
Raritan, 21
Rockingham, 71
Ronckendorff, William, 53
Russell, John Earl, 35-36, 88

St. Louis, 76
San Jacinto, 53
Scott, Winfield, 21
Sea Bride, 63
Semmes, Raphael, 18, 19, 20, 21-30, 36-37, 39-42, 44-56, 58-
    67, 69-74, 76-78, 80-92
Shenandoah, 18, 33,93
Sinclair, Arthur F., 37, 47-48, 66, 71, 83-84, 89
Sinclair, William, 61
Soley, J. Russell (quoted), 33-34

Somers, 21
Spencer, Philip, 21
Sprague, Horatio, 29
Sumner, Charles, 94
Sumter (ex *Habana*), 19, 24-29, 40, 44, 73
Sumter, prizes taken by, 98

Tacony, 18
Talisman, 61
Tallahassee, 33
Tasmanian, 91
Thornton, James S., 87, 93
Tonawanda, 49
Tunstall, T. T., 44
Tuscaloosa (ex *Conrad*), 18, 61-63, 69
Tuscaloosa, prizes taken by, 101
Tuscarora, 35-36
Tycoon, 71

Vanderbilt, 55, 60, 64-65
Vanderbilt, Cornelius, 55

Wachusett, 93
Waddell, James T., 18, 93
Washington, Treaty of, 94
Wave Crest, 49
Welles, Gideon, 51, 52, 61, 89, 92-93
White, David, 50
Wilkes, Charles, 60-61
Wilson, Joseph D., 48
Winslow, John A., 73-74, 76, 81-89, 92-93
Worth, William, 21
Wyoming, 67

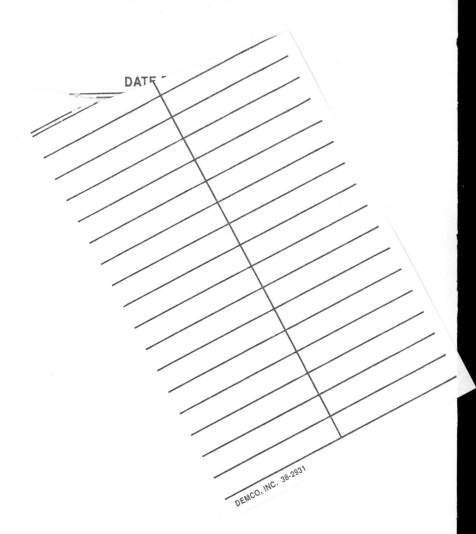

DATE

DEMCO, INC. 38-2931

HAMILTON MIDDLE SCHOOL
139 E. 20TH STREET
HOUSTON, TX 77008